WOMEN PSYCHOLOGY. INSIDE AND OUT

8.575.

It's better for a man not to know what a woman may think about. Just not to know. What you don't know can't hurt you.

3.259.

A man should behave with a woman honestly and courageously, otherwise, she will fall into fear of uncertainty and turn into a witch. Lies and uncertainty create fear in women.

1894.

Women commit considerably fewer crimes than men do.
And it certainly makes them more morally upstanding.
What makes them amoral is the fact that the reasons of most male crimes are usually women.

3.261. Sad woman.

The man is very dangerous to lie to a woman, for faith is love, losing faith, the woman turns into the devil.

4239.

A woman is the main engine for evolution...
It's their task to choose best men for propagation, namely the

ones who possess novelty and perfection. She who chooses the right man as the father for her children, will be loved by destiny.

1588.

Forgive women their little sins. At least 15 days per month they are ruled by hormones. And hormones are an awful thing. It means irritation, conflicts, mood swings, getting offended and crying etc.
But other 15 days it means being another person- a kind, soft and happy one.

9.4024. A whole.

The point of the metaphor of God's creation of Eve from Adam's rib is that the husband should love his wife as he loves himself and that she is the closest person to him. The wife is the one next to the heart.

2023.

Neither a man nor a woman who should set a high value on promises and vows given by a woman. It's all because a woman is responsible not only for herself but also for her children and children are a sacred thing. And no vows should influence their comfort. That's why a person who demands silly promises from a woman, commits a sin and will be punished for it.

8.1306.1.

A woman needs a man who would be able to make her fears disappear.

10.6957. Love me black.

Call a woman a vile monster... she will be outraged at first, and then she will even be pleased. A woman likes to be a monster. A man is one who is monstrous on the outside, a woman is one who is monstrous on the inside.

2800. A demon and his witch.

A woman should be a bit like a witch. She should find her Fiend and ride him. Don't worry as all women can do it... And so do you.

10.6955.

Women divide themselves into cats and chickens. Women are flattered when they are called cats. Women are flattered when they are considered evil, vile monsters.

4315. The source of pain.

A strong independent woman refuses to recognize any authority and control over her. But it's very difficult to find a stronger man who could be able to tame her. Loneliness makes this woman unhappy. Strength brings pain. Strength is the source of pain.

10.6970. Taming a wild Mare.

Don't be afraid to tease a woman, of course, she will be angry and throw herself at you, but if you defeat her, she will automatically fall in love with you.

10.5529.

To bow before women and children is not necessary, it is enough just to love them.

4.853.

They say Venus is a symbol of women, if so, then you can easily understand what kind of hell is going on in women's souls: methane atmosphere, acid rain.

9.3841. In the beginning everybody was propagating by germination.

Who was the first - man or woman? Egg or hen?

5.105.

The Princess and the sex of the Kingdom in addition is a symbol of love. A man who has found his love will find his Kingdom.

5.611.

A woman is looking for a man who could help her escape from herself.

5.732.

The maternal instinct makes a woman automatically love everything beautiful, growing and fruitful.

6.197.

To meet and start a relationship with a girl, you should think about what kind of man she wants and let her know that you are... Think of the feminine male ideal, and become it.

6.305. Hero feat.

A woman's " No "is a" Yes " for the reason that women often tell a man the opposite of what they want to provoke in him the desire to prove the opposite. Women are afraid of their desires and are looking for a hero who can overcome their fears. Or they just know that men all like to do the opposite.

7.270.

Muse this is the woman who inspires his admiration of the hero of the exploits.

7.271.

Too clever women are poorly suited to the role of the Muse, because it is seriously something to admire, and consequently to encourage they do not know.

7.653. Is it me, or have you lost weight?

If you do not know what to say to a woman, with surprise note how she lost weight and looks great.

7.678. An intelligent woman.

The greatest compliment to a woman is praising her intelligence.

7.885. Source of faith.

The weakness of women in uncertainty, so they are very fond of confident men who can and know what they want. A woman needs a man who can compensate for a woman's insecurities.

7.896. Mutually beneficial people.

A man needs a woman to admire him and thus inspire him. A man is useful to a woman in that he allows her to overcome her fears and insecurities, which gives peace and inspires happiness.

7.960.

A woman draws energy from nature, a man-from a woman... Therefore, the better you organize the rest of your woman, the more it will bring you income.

94.

A woman will be very grateful for everything you
do for her...
But once you refuse to do something for her...
the first thousand grateful moments will soon be forgotten.

127.

Men are scared of smart women. The reason is simple. Men know what women want. And a smart woman always gets what she wants. And a man will pay for everything...

293.

On account of total political correctness and tolerance.
I wouldn't divide the people into males and females...

395.

There is a frog in every princess.

4.60.

The easiest way to kill love is to count it in money.

4.89.

Women love a hero, a hero worthy of admiration. Win and the woman will love you. Conquer yourself and your vices. Overcome problems and troubles. Win, achieving goals and realizing dreams.

4.90.

The capacity for ritual is the capacity for love. If a woman sees that a man has dreams and he systematically implements them, then we can hope that he is able to love.

5.80. Consequences of female Masturbation.

The property of a man Onanist – "I want everything at once and quickly", but women do not lag far behind men. Is a woman - a Muse she inspires and helps the hero, and sometimes a woman onaniste, it wants to find a ready-made hero. Such a woman does not understand that the hero loves beauty, not women, so a woman can not attract such a man. Therefore, the woman Onanist attracts the men of onanists, men of unprincipled and little capable of exploits, and such a woman does not know how to inspire.

6.34.

I've been married to the same woman three times. But each time it was a different me and a different woman.

6.55.

Ask a woman what she likes ...for if she likes, she believes.

764. Themis was a woman. [In brevi]

A real woman always feels the good and the bad.

919.

There's something more precious than money ...namely, women.
There's something more precious than women... namely, children.
... even though...

946.

Never criticize your woman... And this way you'll become the most precious one in her life...

9.61. Woman is a source of energy for man.

While chasing a woman, a man makes a lot of useful movements. Movement is life and a source of energy.

969.

A woman can only love the man she can admire,
the one who can protect her...
... being near whom makes her feel honored,
... the one who gives her positive emotions: pleasure, serenity, confidence, warmth.

993.

A perfect woman can tolerate her man's attacks of rage.
Especially those she caused herself...

1523. [In brevi]

If a man becomes a victim of female sexuality, charming nature or flirting, natural instincts evoke inside him and the ability to think straight turns off.

1528.

A woman's desire to score off a man is based on her desire to find the man she won't be able to score off. As women like winners. A woman needs a male she can feel safe being with as she will be able to forget about her eternal fear and lack of confidence.

1536.

Women believe in the « sixth sense» and intuition more than in logic. That's why instead of any logical explanations, it's better tell them «It seems to me that», «I feel that it's right», I'm totally sure, I simply feel that it should be done this way, I got a feeling that..» etc.
Of course, it's necessary to think it all out in advance. Finally, verity means logic, in the first place.

1537.

Women put a great emphasis on looks. If a man wants to impress a woman and make her like him, he should freshen himself up and look clean and neat. Clothes should be clean, nails done, face shaven and shoes shiny.

1540.

When it comes to fighting for a place in the sun, the main tool of a woman is sexuality and womanhood.

1542.

A phone talk with a sweetheart for a woman is not an information transfer act but rather a social act proving the connection between people. That's why in a situation like that a man and a woman can talk about anything at all. The very contact is what matters.

1545.

It's irrational to see a relationship between a man and a woman as opposition or fights. It's more like a mutual symbiosis and helping each other. Having joined once, the two form a whole organism.

1553.

Women are stronger than men. Women have better health, stamina, they are more resilient and stress-resistant. Women's memory serves them better and they are more patient and diligent.
What do they need men for? The thing is that the task of a woman is to survive and give birth. Women are barely risk-taking enough to endanger their wealth. That's why a woman needs a man, a man fighter who (if necessary) would die in a battle, a man-explorer, a man-getter. A man who is able to get into a fight and maybe catch a piece of «a place in the sun» where a woman will soon pleasantly lie in the sun.
Women cultivate tolerance, empathy, tenderness, understanding and womanhood in themselves. All these feelings let women exist successfully, while using men as some kind of sword, a source of wealth, as protection.

1555.

Praise people. Actually people don't get enough praise, not even women. Though they say that women are used to flattery. There are two sides of the same coin. If one doesn't get enough praise, then every time they praise this person will be like a present. And if one gets praised often, then lack of praise may make one feel uncomfortable and hurt. Praise is like a drug that one gets addicted to and can't live without. That's why praise people in any case. Praise is a drug for a person, a real pleasure.

1557.

Usually a typical woman is interested only in herself, relationships and children. While men can have many different interests.
And here lies the root of misunderstanding between men and women. Men don't get why women don't worry about things that seem important to men, while women don't get why men

waste time and efforts on various stuff.

P.S. When we say that a woman is interested only in herself, it also includes everything that is personally important to her: her man, her life, her work, her pleasures, her home, etc.

1568.

A woman can really forgive the man she loves anything at all. As well as a man can forgive the woman he loves for anything. But it doesn't make scandals, screams and mutual reproaches disappear. What's more, it's not even the true reason for a conflict that may kill love but rather heart-to-heart talks it involves.

1571.

Apart from sex, beauty and children, a woman can give a man many other things. For instance, moral support, care, tenderness, compliments, flattery, help with something he does, peace of mind, warmth etc. And what's more interesting, a man really expects it all from a woman and becomes really offended when he doesn't get it. However, women want the same things from a man, plus many other ones. That's why it's all mutual.

1583.

A woman is attracted to a strong man. A woman is attracted to a real man. A woman dislikes it when a man is insincere, lying, weak, unnatural. A woman dislikes when a man tries to seem someone he's not really is. A man should BE but not SEEM to be.
That's why if some man has problems with women and women dislike him, then this man should not blame women for it all. This man doesn't even have to read instructive books about how to amuse women. He only needs to BECOME a man. As it's not external sexual characters that make a man a man but rather some inner soul state and women can feel it. As is known, women live by feelings.

1586.

In the eyes of a woman it's always a man who's to blame for everything. It should be clearly understood.

That's why it's useless for a man to justify his actions and prove he's not guilty. A man only needs to admit his faults, apologize and promise he'll never do it again.

1593.

The natural goal of a woman is to choose the best man among all those available to her. But how and by which means can she do it?

A human being is a social animal. Most people do not tend to think for themselves but rather tend to see the reaction of those around and analyze it to take some decision. That's why sometimes it's not a man himself but women who are close to this man that seem important to a woman. Since a man is liked by other women, thus there's a probability that this man is precious.

Besides, there are also several social stereotypes that can influence the choice, namely TV, mass media, the Internet that forms social preferences. Since they talk about it and write about it, and everyone thinks that THIS is the right thing, then it's true. At least, it's worth being paid attention to. As they don't show bad stuff on tv...

Habits and company. Tastes often get formed in childhood under the influence of some random factors. A curious observation. Imagine some area. And let's imagine that all men in this area are long-eared. And all women have to choose these men (there are no other ones). A young girl who becomes mature in this area, will see that all other women choose such men and their ears will seem a sign of great men to her. But once this girl comes to another country, she may meet short-eared men... An exotic thing of course, but still there's something wrong... How to live with such freaks?

And, certainly, there are some basic criteria like wealth, power, intellect, health, successfulness... No one has repealed classical things.

P.S. By the way, in order to prevent all people from choosing the same, nature invented a great mechanism. Approximately 5-20% of people are nihilistic and choose the opposite. Thus, they look at what others choose and choose the opposite. But it doesn't mean that they make a right balanced decision. Totally not. They simply choose something opposed to what others choose.

And what's more curious. Many people combine these two behavioral manners in themselves. Perhaps, there is some loaded dice inside them so they throw it and take a decision whether to be like others or do things vice versa in a particular situation...

1595. Source of pleasure.

Modern life made it possible for a woman to choose a man not only because of money but also because of his soul and other traits.

Nowadays a woman can make money on her own and can protect anyone. So now it's not only money and power that are important about a man. Now a woman may choose, for instance, a soulmate... or other traits in a man. For instance, kindness, tenderness, care, the ability to be a perfect lover...
It can be said that nowadays a woman needs a man for pleasure...

1596.

There are two ways of thinking, two types of understanding the world:

• Logical thinking - logic typical of male nature.
• Mystically sensual understanding of the world - female way of thinking.

It's a very disputable issue of what way of thinking is better. Men think that it's logic that rules the world. While women say that the world is mystically irrational.

But we know as we remember that the truth in this world is always hidden in balance. In the blend of Yin and Yang, Chaos and Order, Black and White. It should be said that both types of understanding of the world - logic and feelings - taken separately are unable to see the real world view. Only after having become united and formed some symbiosis to use both of the types of understanding, people can see the world as it is. The world where both Rational and IRrational laws take place.

Our world, our reality is rational and irrational at the same time. Some things happen in it according to logical laws and have cause-and-effect connections, while other events and phenomena are caused by its mystical sensual nature. Really, besides logic there exist luck, fortune, karma... There's hardly anyone who would deny it not to jinx it.

Everyone had periods in life called a train of misfortunes and no logic would explain that. And everyone had moments when a run of good luck would eclipse anything. Why can't it be so? And what could not happen under no circumstances, sometimes became real.

1597.

Female mystical sensual way of thinking understands the world through images, emotions, feelings... A woman feels the world around. That's why if a man wants to tell a woman about something, he should talk about his feelings and ideas concerning the subject of the conversation:

Such a nice gorgeous red car. Its color is so warm that you'll like it I guess. It's so comfortable with its warm velvet seats and soft plastic and leather steering wheel pleasant to the touch. The music is nice, the sound is clear and so mellow... A big navigation system with a big screen.
I'm simply sure you'll like this car. You will look great together with it.

1598.

Women are very important for this world. The main benefit of a woman for the world is giving birth and bringing up children. This benefit only is already enough for them to go to paradise. But this is not the only benefit of a woman. There are many other implicit but interesting benefits, for instance: women choose the best males for giving birth. This tendency makes males «turn themselves inside out», become better and figure out anything at all even how to conquer the world only to prove to a woman that one is among the best males worth being a partner for giving birth and nice future. In order to make a woman pay attention to a man he should earn, create, cultivate wits and perfection in himself and try to be better than other men or be noticeable among them. It's a male need that is caused and influenced by a woman and it's a big driving motive that makes this world go round and eternally move forward.

A man has to prove to his beloved woman that he's the best so that she would choose him among a thousand other men. And a man has to work for that.

Of course these are not the only two roles of women. There are many other ones, but discuss it later.

1599.

Women are considered to be the creators of the modern world-building, modern «consumer society». Women create a demand and form preferences. 60% of purchases in the world are effected by women, and perhaps other 30% are for them as well.

Many people who don't fully understand the essence of life and nature of the «consumer society», see it as a negative problem and consider consumer society an evil thing while women are the ones feeding the evil with their never ending desire to buy things.

In fact it's a very big mistake to consider consumer society an evil thing. As this is the society where people CREATE and where there's a place for work... Just so you know, if people don't consume then creating something will be unnecessary and there will be no work and it will result into unemployment, hunger, poverty, devastation. So the balance of creating and consuming is necessary. Our world is permanently on the edge of overproduction crisis and we can't sell everything we produced. We would like to create something but no one needs it. You say that people consume a lot? Absolutely not, as people consume as much as they need or less. Of course consuming is necessary and important. Perhaps it's better to switch to non-material values (like SPA, massage, books, cinema, fitness, games), that demand less of the material values. But however, female desire to buy ...buy... and buy is very important for this world. It gives WORK to those people who WORK and create something. And almost EVERYONE works: both women and men. And each one of us who complains about humble wages and lack of work should remember that it's exactly the consumer society and people's desire to buy that influence it all.

That's why when a woman buys herself another dress or jewellery, don't blame her. Just think how many people and families were made happier and given work thanks to her wishes and desires.

A woman's desires make the world better and more beautiful.

1605.

Perhaps, women do not understand the value of words and words don't mean anything for them. But women understand feelings and really appreciate sincerity. To make a woman understand you, she should feel what you're trying to tell her.

1617.

Women tend to use mimicry. In essence, a woman is the reflection of her man. That's why women look for the best and strong-est men. Once she becomes reflected in a man, she can make her-self much better and stronger too.

It's a known fact that there is a strong woman behind every suc-cessful man. But it can be said vice versa: there is a man behind every successful woman. A woman adsorbs thoughts and intel-lect of men who belong to her...

1619.

A beloved woman should be forgiven for anything and treated like a queen.
Why? Because she's a beloved woman and a beloved one is al-ways a queen.

1627.

Girls become mature quite early, much earlier than boys do. And not to seem strange, they put on masks and pretend to be little girls and habitually stay in this role up to the old age.

1631.

Women are much more stronger and smarter than men. Even because besides her own power and wits a woman may also use all advantages of her man. A symbiosis like this makes a woman a very dangerous opponent. As in fact, while conflicting with a woman one gets into a conflict with a group of people and two can always womp one.

1649.

As is known, men like fantasy while women like detective stor-ies. It's equal to saying that men like to tell stories while women like to tell tales.

1686. By resigning herself to a man, a woman starts to rule over him.

«Victory through defeat». The power of a woman is in her weakness. By being submissive, she makes him submissive. By giving up, she takes him prisoner...

1699.

A woman who gobbles up your time, money and nerves... are probably very hungry. Perhaps feeding her is a good idea?

1891.

A woman's desire to tame a raging animal of a man results from her primal instincts. And the stronger the man and his rage are, the more pleasure a woman will get out of taming him... A weak woman who tamed a Strong man... The stronger he is, the more rage he's got and the nicer a woman feels while taming him. A raging animal wants freedom, but... a female needs the strongest of all males and only after making him tamed she will be happy.

When a woman looks at the best man, she imagines her future children.
These children will be wonderful. As it's exactly her Mr.Right. And it's only him who she will show her real nature to. For others she will always be a monster or a set of masks, but the one chosen by her will get to know her real nature.

2085.

Women tend to be tempted and worship the Devil more.
It happens because titans have super power and they are the best among humans.
And women tend to serve the best and strongest.
A woman is weak on the inside and she needs an external source of power.
Getting energy from this source, she becomes stronger herself.

Perhaps, that's why there are so many women and weak men who work for corporations. As the bosses of these organizations are so powerful that resemble titans.

2108.

A noble woman resigns herself only to her man and tells others
go to hell. While a stupid low woman acts the opposite way.

2115.

A woman wants and admires a strong smart man.
Her instincts simply scream out: I need his power and wits,
.... I will be both strong and smart with him...
No person will ever offend me or laugh at me.
Now everyone will admire me and be scared of me.
And my children... my wonderful children will derive only the
best from both of us...

There is one more demand: he should be kind with her. Firstly,
because we're kind with those we love and secondly, we remember that demons cause pain while noble people are kind.

2123.

There's nothing more precious for a woman than a man who
makes her forget all her fears.

However, on the other hand, to forget is not the word. It resembles an escape. She wants to escape from reality with him.
Women like imagined worlds that they can leave for.

All in all, why not escape but my original concept was the following one: since we live in the real world, no escape will help
us. It's important not to forget fears but to get over them. We
should leave our fears behind but not run away from them.

Though...sometimes it's ok to run away or forget about them...
Everything's possible as long as there's no fanaticism about it.
So, take my hand and let's escape...together into the imagined
world full of palm trees and the sea and let's forget our hum-
drum reality.

2127.

Women are genetically predisposed to feel fear. Fears simply live within a woman.
She should survive by all means and save her children. Any threats or risks are enemies to her nature. A woman is a mother, in the first place. And children are of ultimate importance in her life.

2128.

In olden days it was a man who protected his woman. And now it's work who is the main protector of almost every woman. Women are very devoted to their work. And work is what protects, feeds and helps a woman forget her fears. If only it was possible to start a family with work, men would surely become totally insignificant.

In the world where the functions of a bread-earner, protector, guarantor of stability and deliverer of fears are discharged by work, there are only several useful functions left for men, namely kindness, tenderness, joy and fun. Hence, men are mostly needed for fun and a little for thinking and reproductive activity.

A modern woman hardly sees a man as a protector, bread-earner or a deliverer of fears... – but men miss the olden days. As they used to like how it felt being protectors and heroes, but time made them forget how it should be done.

2195.

A constant demonstration of love is what one really needs.
Love is ethereal. You're constantly in fear of losing it...
And fear brings pain and discomfort so you should overcome it.
Demonstrations of love is what can help you get rid of fears to be happy.

Love is a very precious thing. The presence of love brings pain because one is constantly afraid of losing it. "My dear- you say to it. - You'll be forever mine". But you're talking to an invisible thing and that's why you need demonstrations of it. Otherwise you'll simply go mental from fear and painful feeling that you've lost it.

2204.

She became only stronger with his every betrayal. And finally she got so strong that he no longer seemed necessary to her. As every strong woman needs a man who is even stronger so that to let herself feel cute and weak.

2398.

Girls grow up fast but prefer to pretend childish for a long time. But men may remain children forever while pretending to be grown ups.

2756.

A person who loves a particular goal and never gives up to fulfil it, will surely do it. As goals are like women who fancy assertive men.
When a goal says 'No' it actually means "Maybe". And when it says "Maybe" it means "YES! YES! YES!"

2841.

A perfect woman resembles a lioness. She's strong and brave, and a good hunter with sharp teeth. She respects her lion and listens to him and loves her baby lions. And she sees everyone around as enemies or food and is ready to tear everyone who gets too close to pieces.

2857.

A woman shouldn't change. It's better if she changes dresses...

2903.

Beauty is not the most powerful weapon of a woman.

The most powerful weapon of any woman is tenderness.
A man in love doesn't see or hear anything asa man in love can only feel. And tenderness is the best thing to feel.

2949. Faithfulness and loyalty.

A stupid woman is the one who is vain and weak with complexes. She sees everyone as a judge and wants to serve anyone who praises her or promises protection. She serves her relatives, parents, children, bosses, colleagues, friends, anyone at all including her loved husband. She serves everyone at all. And does it really differ her from a low woman who sleeps with everyone?

While a decent, strong and smart woman serves her man only. And I call it faithfulness and loyalty.

2979.

I like it more when a woman resembles a man rather than when a man resembles a woman. Even if generally I like women more than men.

2980. It's logical.

I especially love women who love me...

2983.

Money is like women who love the strong, the smart and the brave...

2990. Making the complicated simple.

Female brain is quite an interesting device as its logic is so complicated that it's barely understandable. But it's easy to feel it.

Malicious tongues say that there is no woman's reason at all as a female head is only full of feelings. But I disagree. There is some logic there though its laws are random.
Woman's reason is a kind of logic which laws are random and de-

pendent on mood and time of the day.

3000. Order is fear. [In brevi]

Order craves to overcome chaos.

Order is fear. A female soul that is under the control of forces of order, wants to get rid of fear and looks for a man who can kill it. A man to kill the dragon.

She wants victory and power and at the same time she wants to be defeated to gain freedom.

A good girl looks for a bad girl to become a bad girl.

3027. Unpleasant truth [In brevi]

Youth is like male inner self that means chaos and novelty.
Old age is like female inner self that means order and perfection.

Youth doesn't appreciate order while old age doesn't like novelty.

3028.

A woman's need for chaos, novelty and anything forbidden is typical of reproductive age. As soon as a woman solves the issue with progeny, she starts to prefer classical female values like peace, order, safety, patterns and conventionalities. A man also starts to share these values but a bit later, usually 5-10 years later.
P.S. by the way, here lies the problem of middle-aged women's search for partners. Both men and women have the same tastes and values in their youth. But at the age of 30-45 a woman is already a woman, while a man is still a man, and their values differ. Later in life, by the age of 45, a man will gradually lose his male passion for chaos and will share a woman's need for order. Generally, due to progress in medical industry and shift of the reproductive age, all these objective laws may be applied to older age groups.

3081.

It's important to treat a woman with care, blandishments and cajoling. It's a bad idea to influence a woman with power and swearing. On the other hand, the best variant is the one when a woman takes necessary decisions by herself.

It's a perfect variant when no one imposes any will on each other but everyone acts intuitively. A man fosters bodily, will and intellectual power in himself. Then, by using these powers and the ability to search for novelty a man fulfils his goals and plans, that will bring him money and power.

Women like men who possess uniqueness, intellectual and will power, money and influence. A woman herself wants to possess a man of this kind and serve him. While a man wants to possess and serve a woman who has beauty and the ability to provide him with extra energy like care, tenderness, love. When each of them starts to cultivate things they love in each other, their partnership will be strong and unbreakable and no one will have to talk anyone over. In essence, a woman doesn't need much from a man. If a man can provide her with a good house, bringing up children and support for his woman, and also gives her care and tenderness...such man will seem perfect in the eyes of the woman and she will do anything he wants without any unnecessary promises.

By the way, it's not necessary for a smart woman to look for a man who already has money and power. She only needs to find a man who is strong in will, mind and body. And then love this man and provide him with special power, the power of love. This power will help a man raise and achieve success, power and wealth. All it takes is mutual love and the state of being aimed at achieving success together.

3084.

The main value of a woman in the eyes of a man is not only sex and children but also care, tenderness and moral support.

As well as something non-material which I call "karma and good luck". When a person serves perfection, this person's karma becomes better.

3160.

There's hardly anyone who can torment a woman more than another woman.

3203. The Venus de Milo.

A light imperfection of something perfect makes it even more wonderful.

3205.

Female beauty was made to make men serve and worship them, in order to protect women and provide them with resources for «building a nest and growing nestlings».

That's why everything about female beauty is very precious. Worshiping female beauty is a natural state of things. Even female desire to change worships the beauty. Such a changeability helps women keep their weapon on alert not to let men get used to it. And nature encourages women to the right actions by giving them pleasure when it comes to taking care of their beauty. Beautiful hairdos, make up, cosmetics, clothes and shoes give women great joy.

3206. Money uses women in order to be embodied.

It's mostly beautiful women who manage to embody money well. A beautiful woman is kind of a magnet that attracts money from all directions so that to spend it soon and embody it in the real world. And we remember that the essence of money existence is in its desire to be transformed into something material out of air. This quality typical of women can be used by their husbands in different ways. On the one hand, a beautiful wife is a talisman that attracts money into the family. On the other hand, a wife may take money out of her husband's pocket, bringing the family budget down.

The important thing here is to put this magnet in the right place so that it would attract money from the outer world (perhaps through a husband's pocket). Such a pump may inject good money out of external reality into a family budget.

The right strategy in this direction is about paying for a woman's desires from present or future income, without getting into debts or savings. It's necessary to make the magnet attract the good from the external world and not exhaust any supplies. It's important not to get into debts or supplies and it will make a woman a great talisman for attracting money.

3236. Uniqueness is always beautiful.

There are no unattractive women but there are women who are alike.

3240.

I don't like fairy tales but I like it when life resembles a fairy tale.

3.249.

The woman next to the insecure man falls into fear in Cuba, she is overcome by suspiciousness, paranoia, hysteria and anger.

3.250.

The uncertainty of men creates in the woman a witch.

3.255.

If a man torments a woman with uncertainty and fear, a woman subconsciously wants to send him to hell and leave. The point is, if she leaves and he is left without the love that is God, he will instantly fall into hell and go crazy. And if it doesn't and will not fail, therefore, love was not in it so especially it is not needed.

3.256.

Weak woman frightening alongside weak and uncertain a man, to overcome fear, she turns into a witch.

3.257.

The fear and uncertainty of a man turns a woman into a witch, because fear is the devil, and a witch is a woman of the devil.

3.262.

A man who has no God turns a woman next to him into a devil. What is God? God is power, faith, hope, love, determination, courage. In short, you can not lie, doubt, fear and sit idle.

3.264.

A well-meaning woman can lie and a man can't. Men lie kills the woman's faith, filling it with despair and suspiciousness. Hypocrisy breeds jealousy, hysteria, anger, etc.

3.265.

You can't lie to someone you love. Love is fusion, not multiplication. You lie to the woman you love, you increase her fear and suspiciousness tenfold.

3.271.

A man lies to a woman from the best motives, she believes, but then expectations are broken and there is a cognitive dissonance. A lie begets fear, and fear as grebes climb the germs of suspicion. Suspiciousness is hysteria and jealousy. The man turned the woman into a witch, and then he cries.

3283. Sellout partners.

Women who see men only as a source of money, attract only those men who see them only as a source of sex.

3.454.

Man is chaos. The woman, simplifying the man, forces him to come down to earth, turns chaos into order.

3.559.

People, particularly women, don't like wankers, wankers because it's deceitful, stupid, lazy and cowardly individuals who don't love anyone but himself.

3579. Female intuition.

A woman may not understand some things but she feels everything.

Some may blame women for their twisted logic but perhaps it's an advantage rather than a fault. A woman doesn't need to think as she feels at once whether something is right and good or wrong and bad. Since time immemorial women have been busy with picking, and their main task was to feel and decide whether a particular thing is good or bad. It doesn't take any logic to realize it as it should be felt to be good or bad.

While men were hunters and hunting demands logical networks and observation. Men needed feelings too, but not as much as women did.

Anyone who is looking for something and craves to find it, should trust female intuition. Any dilemma that demands realizing whether something is good or bad, can be solved by female intuition as it's a very useful tool. And searching and finding is originally a female activity.

Again, one should realize that female intuition typical of a searcher and male logic typical of a hunter is not
an axiom, but rather an evolutionary mechanism that took a million years for its development. It only concerns the inborn strong traits typical of the Searchers and the Hunters. Women can also use logic and men can trust their own intuition, but there is a matter of preponderance of some skills over other ones. As sometimes women should hunt as well and men should

do picking or husbandry.

A woman is the best oracle and she only needs to feel whether something is good or bad.
A man is the best strategist who is able to figure out the plan of hunting.

Intuition is a sensual way of understanding that helps to feel whether something is good or bad.
While logic is the way of understanding that helps to use some known factors to realize whether something is good or bad. Logical way definitely works when some facts are known. But do we really know enough facts and details?

Intuition has its errors, but it's often more effective than logic. And any logic can be deceived by false facts. Logic demands attention and time to study enough facts. Something left un-noticed may give the reason for a well-founded building of logical thoughts to tumble down.

The best way of understanding is to use both logic and intu-ition.

By the way, have you ever noticed that people choose what they lack. And women, originally weak in logic, like to read detectives. Detectives are their food for thought, like a living teacher and master helping them to upgrade the weak skill. And the alphabet of the Searcher as well. A detective is someone who searches for evidence and proof in order to find some goal. Hence, it involves many traits typical of a Picker. It's import-ant to find enough evidence. Searching and finding the truth is originally a female pleasure. Assembling puzzle pieces into the whole picture is a task really entertaining for women.

Men are not fond of searching as they prefer to chase and catch. They don't want to assemble puzzle pieces but prefer to figure out how to catch a whole Mammoth.

3.627.

A man, gradually bringing a woman closer, accustoms her to him to the extent that she becomes uncomfortable and anxious without him.

3.655. A cure for uncertainty.

When a man lies or scares a woman, he automatically turns her into a witch. Lies, anger, weakness and lack of confidence men give rise to uncertainty, a wonderful nourishing environment in which women's rising fears. Fear turns a woman into a witch. Trying to conquer uncertainty, a woman devours a man.

3.686.

Cowardly men have erection problems. They are so afraid of women that the blood goes to their feet and paralyzes the brain. That's why women do not like cowards, sex with them is bull-shit.

3740. [In brevi]

For a modern woman, work can be a substitute for a man. But not a complete substitute.

3868.

The main task of a woman is to inspire her man to heroism.
A woman should be a muse and a source of inspiration for her man.
But the desire to be a ghoul or an idol results from the same source that the apple core known as the reason for people's ex-pulsion from the paradise, once did...

3869.

A perfect woman is not a holy ghoul but rather a muse and a helper, as well as a source of care, gentleness and support.
Look for a really nice woman and don't waste your time on ghouls.

3909. It's you.

Her face is hidden beneath masks and birds live in her heart.

3912. A symbol of power.

The goddess in a cat mask whose Power instills fear and envy. They go to her to learn how to live.

3913. A condescending haughtiness wearing a mask and a red dress.

Beauty sublimes and gives strength. Masks are bare of fear. Haughtiness is her only weakness but we like even her faults.

3940. A woman is form and a man is content.

A relationship between a man and a woman is a relationship between form and content... A relationship between a jug and water. Chaos taking the form of order. A woman is a form and a man is content. They are two inseparable interacting matters.

A woman is order and a man is chaos. Chaos strives for order and order strives for chaos. It's not even a symbiosis but two inseparable matters like form and content. Content deprived of any form may turn into a puddle and fade away, and an empty contentless form is almost an intangible thing.

4048.

A man should be hellbent but it's necessary to bend him in the right direction.

4.125.

Too cowardly and weak woman will greatly love her child, turning him into a neurotic. She will love him in order to bind herself from intense fear for her "overvaluation". Such mothers oversee the baby.

4127.

The nature of desires is such that he who wants too much will get too little. Thus, desires resemble women. It's dangerous to want too much even from one of them, and if one wants too many, they will all get offended and leave.

4.149.

When a woman sees an immature and weak man, she instinctively feels attracted to him, because at the level of the subconscious feels that if you warm the chicken with your love, it can grow into a great cock.

4175. A recipe for success.

Foster fanaticism in your nature and be faithful to your desires up to the end.

Desires resemble women: they like faithfulness and bring faithful people luck and joy. But those who leave things undone and often get passing fancies... are very disliked.
Besides, the weaker a desire is, the stronger the laziness... It's laziness that stops a person from fulfilling goals. There are no unachievable goals. But desires can be so weak that laziness overcomes them.

4.200.

After the birth of a child, a woman concentrates love on him, and her husband is very in love limits, the meaning of this maneuver to provoke her husband to sublimation of sexual energy to creative, make him work and make a career. If the husband grows up and pays attention to the child, the woman will retain sexual interest in him.

4209. A happy person looks beautiful.

Happiness becomes her. Happiness makes her prettier.

4218. Take care of a woman.

A woman as means of production, is quite an expensive high-tech being that needs to be properly operated. Crooked hands can disable her really soon.
*

A woman needs a good owner. A woman without her owner is unhappy.
*

A beautiful woman needs an owner, beauty should be protected.
Beauty is a treasure. An ownerless treasure will be stolen soon.

4226. Beauty costs much.

A beautiful woman resembles a luxurious house which everyone would like to have so that she should cost much. Her price is a matter of prestige. The more expensive she is, the better her owner will be. The more he pays for her, the longer he will appreciate her and take care of her. Beauty deserves the best, it needs good hands.
 - An important moment - what is meant here is a buyer, the motives of leaseholders are totally different.

4.229.

The woman, wanting to rule over men, forever leaves his immature childlike state. To Mature, a man must avoid them for a long time, otherwise he will remain a child forever. A man's dependence on a woman turns him into a child.

4231. A free woman.

An independent woman who gained freedom and doesn't have an owner anymore.
But now she has tenants though they are of little use...

Tenants' indifference makes her feel unhappy.
Tenants are unable to love her home..as their own.
Temporary people can only bring destruction.

Having many owners is the same as not having an owner at all.

4307. A very strong woman.

A man surpasses a woman at least because a woman can only fall for a man who she admires and feels like being submissive with...Thus, there is always some man who is stronger than any stronger woman. A woman who is too strong to find a stronger man, is doomed to being single.

4323. The mother of God.

The mother of a new God. The main predestination of a woman is to create a new God. Providence likes people who fulfill their purposes.

The sweetheart of God. The mother of a new God and a new Goddess. The Goddess loved by her God.

4334.

They never leave good women as a good woman is a really precious thing and there are no fools to throw valuable things around.

4.448.

A man only seems, that he wants sex, money and power. In fact, he wants children, and for that he wants the love and admiration of women who would love him and give birth to his children. However, the woman wishes same.

4.587.

The woman feels that something is missing or something extra. However, that is exactly what she does not know. Remember, a woman feels the truth, not knows it.

4.593. Fear is love in reverse.

A woman should know that her brain is so arranged that she often confuses fear with love. She thinks she loves, but in fact, she's just afraid of being alone.

4.596. The main motive of love.

When a woman is scared, she falls in love with the first one who is ready to save her from fear. If a woman is good and has something that protects her from fear, she has no need and it is difficult to love.

4.714.

The woman should follow my feelings than reason, and the man is better to follow the mind than the senses. But remember that many women and men seem to be mixed up in bodies.

4.748.

Women feel and don't like false men. A lying man does not do or say what he thinks.

4.783.

Remembering the tale of the goldfish, every man should always remember the pathological female greed and vanity. If a woman to give vent to her forever just will not be enough.

4.848.

The woman is that part of the man which separates him from the Kingdom of light and the attainment of perfection. To conquer a woman, a man must conquer himself and his passion. He should achieve humility loss. Yes, his Ego requires unity with a woman to restore the integrity of his Ego, but the achievement of this integrity will close the light before him, will close the path of perfection. A woman makes a man a slave to the senses.

4.893.

For a man, a woman can be useful in the sense that, driving him crazy, make him run away from the pain, feeling his inferiority, begin to improve. A woman is an eternal reason for a man to feel his inferiority.

4.894.

It is said that the woman was created from the rib of a man and since then a man, feeling his inferiority and inferiority, is forced to either run after women or strive for self-improvement and creation. Men pick stupid women, and smart sublimate the energy of the libido into the achievement of personal perfection out of a woman.

4.895.

On the other hand, even if a man tries to get rid of his inferiority through a woman, it is unlikely that he will succeed. The device of a woman is such that she knows how to make a man feel his inferiority. Moreover, we believe that the very essence of women's existence is to make men flawed and to deprive them of complacency. A self-satisfied man, devoid of a sense of inferiority, is a defective and lazy man, of no use. The man was normal, he needed the stimulus of growth.

4.909.

Emancipation transforms one woman in the rebellious woman, the evil warrior born of evil, the other turns into a slave. The cause is in extremes, one extreme begets the other extreme. Strong begets weak, the owner makes a slave.

5.357.

A woman is like a strange cheese in a mousetrap. Strange this cheese from the fact that it is not there, and he you are not eating but just sitting on you like a dog in the manger, would not let anyone close... and only barks. As cheese can bark? "No one knows.

5.416.

When a man makes a breakthrough, he is waiting for a collision with someone who will slow him down. Hardness of the man, meeting after breakthrough softness of the woman, gets bogged down in a bog.

5.422.

Success in many areas of human life of men with homosexual orientation is due to the fact that they managed to avoid the trap of female softness, restraining male hardness. In the absence of female resistance, male hardness was able to grow into the sky, and serve beauty without unnecessary interference. A homosexual is essentially a celibate monk whose strength lies in avoiding the swamp of feminine softness.

5.542.

A wife will not obey or love her husband if she does not admire him. Woman is the embodiment of love, whose purpose is to serve beauty. Not in the power of women to love, what there is of beauty or desire for her. The only thing that can save such a marriage is a joint love and attention to children.

5.694. Crooked path.

When a woman has no one to love and no one to admire, she falls into depression and becomes an easy victim of passion.

6.111.

It is very useful for a man to let a woman know that she can control him. However, if the woman do, their Union will be strong.

6.145. He's pleased.

Therefore, a woman does not tell a man what she wants, that a woman is the sun, and a man is an ear of wheat reaching for the sun and its grains are a gift to the sun. But does the sun need this gift? Yes and no.

6.173.

Let rock know. He's dealing with a Man. If you want to win, let him look for someone else.

6.304. Runaway Cinderella.

When a woman has long hinted to a man on a close relationship and he finally reciprocated, the first time it will overcome the horror. If he doesn't like it, he'll run away, and she runs away from that fear.

6.310.

Neurotic people concentrate their passion 100%. Neurotics do not love themselves and therefore 100% dependent on external love, giving everything, they want to get everything in return. The woman is neurotic, dangerous to men, she, throwing him 100% of his love, calls the addiction makes the addict, binds to itself very strongly. And these relationships will be permeated with eternal scandals, because to keep 100% of the tension of love for a long time will not work, there is an addiction and that passion is not lost, the couple is forced to maintain a contrasting background, forever swearing. Since the neurotic cannot share his love when the child is born, the mother will give 100% of her love to the child, and her husband will cool off. And then the husband, dying of drug withdrawal, will begin to run after her and get angry. Baby from overheating love too spoiled. Further, when a neurotic return to work, he will focus fully on either work or will divide yourself between work and child. And, rather, work, because the child, burned by love, will turn into a monster.

6.312.

To control a neurotic, you must control his passion, not allowing him to get too close, you must keep your distance, letting him close, not when he wants, but according to the schedule. Keeping the fire of hope and faith in him that he will not be deceived in receiving his joy. Neurotics cannot be deceived. All people, especially women, are neurotic to some degree, and the degree of neuroticism depends on the balance of love for oneself and the outside world, the number of its joys.

6.339. An angel is a terrible power.

A woman's weakness is in her fear and lies. If you can't remove its defects, it will turn into an invincible monster.

6.381.

Any business start with a compliment, especially if it is a conversation with a woman.

6.521.

Do not confuse courage and stupidity, women love smart, and fools love only fools.

6.749. Energy loves beauty, and beauty loves money and power.

In the concept of YIN and YANG, nothing is a man-pure energy, and beauty is a woman-something that inspires energy and gives it life.

6.863. Unwelcome.

Love is desire. The unwelcome is all that there is no love for. Therefore, it is very important for women that a man wants her. And you'll lose everything you don't want.

7.108.

If you love, serve, love is service. The easiest way to serve is to pay, you can pay with money, time, services. For example, to love the homeland is, first of all, means to pay taxes. To love God is to sacrifice for the Church. To love a woman to put her money. To love your job is to devote all your time and energy to it.

7.219.

Some women are not descended from monkeys, but from gods

and are called goddesses. For normal people it is better to avoid such women, because interspecies sex is a perversion.

7.236. Love for children.

Women love to serve their children, but they are bored to serve alone and they demand the same from men, but men do not understand this service and do not need it, which causes great conflicts in families.

7.242.

The man on every woman's "no" needs to say solid men Yes, but otherwise he was not a man at all.

7.243.

If you love a woman, she will always be beautiful. No magic here, just love distorts the perception of reality in a better way.

7.448.

Women are socially useful, they make men work.

7.640.

It is even easier for women to make compliments than for men. Tell a woman she's smart, looks good, or has lost weight, and she'll be extremely happy.

7.900.

If you're a man, avoid women who don't believe in you. If you are a woman, avoid men who cannot be trusted and who do not believe in themselves.

8.275.

The more "independent" a woman is, the more she is hell-bent on her relationships with men.

8.276. Greed.

Most women are dissatisfied with their men.

8.280. But sometimes it's necessary to do the opposite.

The more praise a woman gets, the better she works. But it's the opposite with men.

8.293.

Many women think about relationships so much that it's interesting whether they devote time to it too.

8.319. Women like the smart.

Beautiful women is a luxury and it takes deep thinking about financial matters to pay for them.

8.332.

Female emotions are the strongest in the first moment and then they fade away ... while it's the opposite with male ones.

8.338.

Emotionality and categoricalness of young women can be explained by the fact that they lack time and have to be quick at choosing the right man among all variants and thus, they have to say no to wrong ones really soon.

8.383. Hunter instinct.

Some feel like chasing something that runs away.

8.572.

A man needs a woman. A woman is a source of joy. On the other hand, it's not every woman who is a source of joy. Besides, there are many other joys and that's why think a hundred times before you get a joy in the face of a woman.

8.580. The essence of muse.

A woman, as a source of desires, is meant to defeat male laziness.

8.606.

Most commonly female aggression results from women's desire to find a magician to fulfil their desires but they meet only talkative tale-tellers. And unfulfilled desires bring great pain, by the way.

8.611.

Girls who like noodles, have problems with weight.

8.612.

Love for noodles is not a matter of stupidity but rather a matter of greed...

8.614.

Desires are like women as they dislike being numerous. A desire can be easily fulfilled when it's the only one and loved thing.

8.615.

Dashed desires are the result of inflated expectations. When someone wants too much.

8.623.

One of the most favorite female activities is to make some mishappening up and then be sad with it.

8.637.

It's only a stupid woman who dreams of becoming a man's meaning of life. The task of any woman is to find a man who already got some meaning of life and become his muse on his way to fulfilling his dream.

8.648.

There's a desire to be a real man near a real woman.

867.2.

It's essential for a woman to be proud and respectful towards her man to love him.

867.3.

Only love can make a woman put up with all her man's faults.

8.755.

A woman who stopped to inspire her man at his goals and deeds, will soon have to look for a new man.

8.816.

The more innocent a woman seems to be, the more potentially dangerous she really is.

8.864.

A man should not be miffed at a woman because she's just a woman. A woman should not be miffed at a man because he's just a man. It's only rational to be miffed at those of the same sex as you are.

8.884.

It's possible to forgive a real woman for all her faults.

8.885.

A man can barely resist a woman who holds control over her sexiness.

8.890.

Female conscience is a myth aimed at hiding female consciencelessness.

8.894.

A woman is potentially stronger than a man as she is able to seduce or inspire him into doing anything.

8.900.

The only handicap that can stop a woman from getting a man is another woman.

8.992.

It's important to marry only a woman who you can be proud of. The same can be said about choosing a husband.

9.320.

A man should never deal or live with a woman who does not believe in him.

9.398.

If you can't deal with a woman, you'd better avoid her company.

9.472. Mantis female.

Men should be protected from women. Girls are exceptionally dangerous for men and can easily eat them up.

9.523.

You don't need to chase women. Firstly, it's a sexual imposition and secondly, better let them chase you.

9.583. Empathy or Imagination?

Empathy is mostly a feminine feature whose biological objective is children up-bringing and adaptation to her sexual partner. In case of men, empathy is more harmful than useful. Men are warriors and heroes. Narcissism and their own emotions are more inherent to them. Attempts to impose empathy upon men make them extremely feminine and of little use for generation.

It is believed that a person's head contains either empathy or imagination. These two features of human soul are in one place. Either you tune yourself to the other person or you resort to imagination.

9.610.

A man needs a woman to maintain contact with reality.

9.619.

Why do you need a woman? Do you have time to spare and a lot of money to waste? Why do you need children? Who are you to reproduce yourself? What is the use of your being in this world? So, first, find your use, then reproduce!

9.626.

it's dangerous to let a woman be alone. loneliness spoils a woman.

9.710. Shrek.

Women are monsters who wear masks, while men don't wear masks... Men are beautiful the way they are.

3.1128. Save the Princess.

Work is like a beautiful woman. Than it more beautiful the more afraid of her and afraid to even approach. Beautiful woman such a lonely Princess waiting for the brave knights. The same goes for work. If you like the job, don't be afraid of it. Be brave and the heart of beauty will be yours.

3.1131.

You should treat your work like a woman, someone who knows how to communicate with women will understand me. On the other hand, the main thing here is love. Those who know how to love men, too, can apply their skill in a career.

3.1271.

The signs are very visible and look like a naked woman lying on the couch, pretending like just like that. Not to notice the sign can be fear, stupidity or criminal carelessness. By the way, signs are very offended if they do not notice...

3.1274. Saw the sign, move fast.

The sign is a naked woman looking at you invitingly. Having seen a sign, you have to act boldly and then you are waited by mad sex. If you are afraid, Providence will be very much offended with you.

3.1275.

Luck is the naked woman in front of you, shamefacedly lowering her eyes. Luck loves the bold and the beautiful. Cowardly and stupid will say, " Luck, why are you standing here naked." Bold will say nothing, but pounce on luck with kisses and take possession of it.

3.1310.

Jealousy is a woman's great weapon to control weak and insecure men, turning them into her slaves.

3.1458. Lust for power.

Pride and lust for power makes women love weak men. A woman is not afraid of a weak man and it fills her soul with pride.

3.1684. Catharsis.

Provoking conflict, a woman provokes a storm. When the storm is exhausted, the man will begin to feel remorse and try to make amends. Storm is useful, it helps to relieve stress and achieve peace of mind.

3.1929. Squirrel in the wheel of love.

A woman, feeling a lack of love, provokes a conflict and a break with a man. Male idealist, encountering such an obstacle, awakens his fire again and wins the woman. Having won the woman, the man again cools down and everything repeats in a circle.

3.1930. God is love.

"If you love me badly, I will eat you," says the woman to her God. A man who loves knows that if he does his job badly, the devil will go mad.

3.1956. Eternally dissatisfied woman, and idealistic.

Men are idealists doomed to a scandalous conflict society and women. For nothing will keep such a man near a woman, except the knowledge of his inferiority and remorse.

3.1957. Negative woman.

Women idealists are characterized by perpetual dissatisfaction with life and the absurdity of nature. Particularly well these women converge with idealistic men. In the conflict of their eternal scandals and abuse is hidden the unity of their love.

3.1958. More hell.

Women idealisti looking for ideal love and find it in the men idealists. However, since the ideal is a lie and illusion, these relations are highly specific and resemble hell, then heaven...

3.1960.

Female idealist who is looking for perfect love, finding that in the man's face instantly idealist falls into hell. Let's be honest, good riddance to both of them.

3.1966.

An idealist woman, when she criticizes an idealist man, intuitively does the right thing. More than anything, the idealist is afraid not to live up to the ideal. Remorse compels such a man to generally maintain the status quo. The main thing to make sure that he did not escape from reality, for example, alcoholism. Ideally, it is desirable to run him to work. However, you should avoid overkill, otherwise the gene will be offended and run away in the bottle...

3.1967. A grain of sand.

The metaphor of a Genie living in a bottle, is a metaphor for men and women Gina shell, which, freeing the Genie out of the bottle, offers him to become a pearl in the shell.

3.1986.

Man and woman idealists is the two fire, which is cold, and to warm up, they bask each other. The main thing in this matter is to keep a distance.

3.2043.

The female personality is a conglomerate of personalities, dependent on external circumstances. Under each of her circumstances and roles, a woman creates her own personality. All these individuals interact with each other and fight for power, trying to recreate the circumstances that gave rise to them.

3.2065. Chameleon and butterfly.

A woman is a chameleon and a man is a balloon. The woman with all the different and her a lot, but man it's a butterfly that knows that she's a worm.

3.2257. The worst fear.

The moon is a metaphor for a woman, because every woman has a dark side of the moon, always hidden from the eyes. The woman is terribly afraid that someone will see her dark side, finds out her most "terrible secrets". But in fact nothing special, Moon and Moon. Whoever was on the moon will understand.

3.2258. The less you know, the better you sleep.

If you compare the relationship of men and women as a metaphor of the Earth and moon, we can see that the man is fully opened, then the dark side of the moon always remains a mystery.

3.2458. And if defeat pride?

A strong woman is doomed to loneliness. Overcoming her fears, she falls into pride and loses the ability to love.

3.2709.

Women are quite afraid that they will have nothing to say, so with a chatty man she will be comfortable in the early stages.

3.2767.

Strong women subconsciously like weak men, because in contrast to them, they increase their self-esteem. A weak man feeds a woman's pride.

4.1050.

A man can possess a woman only by giving her up. A man's attempt to possess a woman turns him into her slave.

4.1099. Woman's nature.

Love your side of the moon, but don't go on the other side of the moon. Love the moon as it is. The phases of the moon is the law of nature, that is the Moon.

4.1143.

Women are more realistic than men. Reason? They're perfect. Men are more aware of their inferiority, more fantasize and soar in the clouds. Dreams make men grow.

4.1167. When you want to get married.

A woman likes to provoke a man's attention with jealousy, when she wants to attract attention or force him to act actively to preserve the relationship.

4.1208.

Unhappy and weak men remind women of children. Women like to take care of children. Women don't like children growing up. Women do not really want anything from the child and prefer to love him for what he is. However, when the child begins to grow up, they begin to demand from him more and more. The instinct of motherhood is the instinct of power, the instinct of narcissism and the thirst for love.

4.1210.

It is good for a woman to have several children. The woman is selfish and does not want to lose her power, does not want to release the child. However, as children are born, she will evolutionarily let go of the adult child and turn her love to the little one. When children become a lot she is not physically able to control them and she would have to accept the loss of power.

4.1226.

Women like to have a lot of friends, it increases their self-esteem.

4.1227.

A woman in a relationship can't just walk away. With other men she would be uncomfortable and anxious. Having quarreled with her man, she can like a Prince from Cinderella rush to seek her love, but it will not be that and it will not be so.

4.1263.

Every woman has or has had a personal maniac that increases her self-esteem.

4.1314.

We doubt that a man, in the presence of his wife, can attain the perfection of the spirit. The woman will demand from him entertainment and money for children. On the other hand, if the man already reached great perfection and a woman, falling in love, they will be delighted, then she is ready to take over the work and finances only with joy and admiration to be there, basking in its rays as the sun.

4.1402.

More than anything, a woman loves when something beautiful grows and increases.

4.1442.

They say baldness is a sign of debauchery and voluptuousness. Libertines suffer from baldness more often than other men. I wonder why?

4.1503.

Women are weak and can cope only with small children. Men are strong, but their strength is a mask under which small children hide.

4.1522.

Passionate and loving man is not suitable for a serious relationship, because, accustomed and sated with love, he will fall out of love and run away to look for another woman. You need a man who's in love with his dream. If you share his dream with him, he, like a mother who loves her child, will love the woman who will share his love with him.

4.1526.

A woman does not love a man at once for much, but loves him for one thing. However, many other people behave in the same way. A lot of bad only emphasizes one good thing.

4.1530.

A woman rejoices when she is wanted. A woman's happiness is when he wants it. When a woman want, she is happy and wants something in return... What does she want? - Different and all in due time. Sometimes to bask in the sun, sometimes to work in the garden, sometimes to throw firewood in the fireplace. A woman likes a status of your own happiness, intuitively she tries to support him. A woman likes to be wanted. A man likes to want. What could she do to make him want her? - Attract attention.

4.1693.

Scenario "frigid woman" is a scenario where the wife does not admire her husband, and her husband goes crazy. In this situation the woman will subconsciously avoid sex, provoking scandals, and on the basis of the offense to refuse sex. At the same time, the scandals will be formally won by a man, which will increase his self-esteem. That is, everyone will get what he wanted: one will avoid sex, the second will amuse his ego. And in parallel, the scandal will underestimate the self-esteem of a frigid woman, and the fact that a man will not leave her, will strengthen it, tying these two even more to each other.

4.1694.

Scandal relieves sexual tension. Not allowing scandal to happen and avoiding it, the man can provoke the woman on sexual interest. A man who keeps calm, equanimity and detachment, invariably remains interesting for a woman.

4.1695.

A frigid woman is a woman who does not admire her man, fears him, considers him a fool, or despises him. And a man can be aggressive, but aggression is a sign of weakness and a woman will be both afraid of him and despise.

4.1715.

Many questions and not questions at all, but a call to action. "Do you want to kiss me?"what is it?" the woman asks. And the man instead of answering, " do you want to?"he takes her and kisses her. Manipulation?

4.1749.

The symbol of the red riding Hood is a symbol of a woman over-loved in childhood. Red riding Hood is a symbol of passion. The wolf is a symbol of the victim of passion, a symbol of men who love men. The wolf is a symbol of what can result in a passion for the greedy and stupid men.

4.1750. The story of one divorce.

Little red riding Hood was looking for a passionate love, as strong as the one that her grandmother loved her. Such passionate love was a wolf. The problem is that passion and wants to have a wolf as a result of passion swallowed little Red riding Hood. Red riding Hood did not like the passionate love of the wolf, in the end she called the hunters. The wolf was gutted and the woman moved back in with my parents.

4.1792.

If the girl is particularly fierce with you feuding, then you can safely admit to her love. With a woman, where there is hate, there is love.

4.1796.

The little mermaid can be seen as the image of a woman who suffers from love, but can not confess love. The little mermaid is mute, the Declaration of love stuck in her throat. Falling in love, she suffers and suffers, walks as barefoot on razor blades. As a result, the Prince goes to another, and this neurotic young woman drowns in a pool with his head. Sad, but fair story, because to commit suicide because you do not want to be friends – a sin.

4.1797.

Observing the little Mermaid, we accidentally noticed that she is, in fact, neither fish nor meat, that is, the classic frigid woman. First she lived in a world of illusions, then the real world she was hurt, to speak of his love she can't, and the Prince kisses only on the forehead. In this woman there is nothing sexy, Prince sex, and the little Mermaid, according to her mentality, focused on ritual dances of the sea and lay their eggs.

4.1817.

In the" Scarlet flower " beauty is a favorite daughter, that is, a child over-loved by the Pope, who will now compare all men with the standard love of his father. All men were monsters to her now, compared to her father. A woman herself can not find love next to her, she does not like anyone. Time passes, the girl stayed at home, she is sadder and sadder. Sad and father, seeing such a negative scenario. Resolution of the scenario is classic: the father chooses her husband away from the house. In the book, this situation occurs under the pressure of external circumstances, but we know that subconsciously a person is looking for exactly those circumstances that help him fulfill his true desires.

4.1824.

The fairy tale "Ruslan and Lyudmila", as well as many similar ones, describe the rite of conquest by a knight of the Princess's heart. To achieve the love of a woman, the hero must perform the feat and save the Princess from all her problems. In real life, a Bargain can be work and the head of the woman, her parents, her current husband.

4.1825.

The images of Chernomor, the monsters in "The Scarlet Flower", Koshchei, the wolf in "Little Red Riding Hood" are all the images that a girl, beloved by her parents, feels in her husband when she gets married. This image is illusory, but the girl perceives it as reality, is afraid of it, hates it and wants to escape. To do this, she needs a new hero who will kill the gray wolf and set her free. In severe cases, this scenario cultivates a model of behavior in a woman aimed at happiness only in the second marriage. The first marriage serves to gain freedom from the parental family, and the second - to get rid of the monster. However, if, after escaping from the first monster, it is carried back to the parents, then the second husband will also be a monster, and the third. Parents who tend to love their daughters in the name of true love for them should expel them from paradise, forcing them to create their own paradise. You can not let the girl run away from the monster to herself. If she runs, then let him run wherever he wants, but not to his parents.

4.1826.

In "Scarlet flower" we see that at some point the beauty still ran away to her parents, but love and suffering still managed to turn the tide. Man to take his wife away to her parents, must show love, tenderness, compassion, etc. to show Aggressiveness, it is better to replace it with a humble suffering and hints that to live without it.

4.1827.

The little mermaid (Sirens) wants eternal soul, she doesn't need a Prince, she wants to create a soul. In real life, this is expressed in a woman's desire to get pregnant and give birth to a child. Such a woman first sacrificially and passionately falls in love with a man, and after receiving a child, love instantly dies, realizing the metaphorical death of the little Mermaid and the birth of a new soul.

4.1831. Swallow-a symbol of hope and the beginning of spring.

After leaving his parents ' house, Thumbelina first falls into the swamp, and then into the darkness of the dungeons. Out of the fire and into the fire, each man is worse than the last. And we see that every time the decision to choose a husband is not the woman herself, but someone else. For it always someone trying to decide what to choose and offer her hell. As a result, gaining strength, the girl makes a bold decision and runs away on her rescued swallow. Thumbelina found someone she could help and warm with her love, in gratitude swallow saves her, opening the door to new opportunities.

4.1832.

The tale of Thumbelina is a story about a woman who never grew up, left to live in a fairyland of elves and beautiful flowers. It is possible that the story of the elf Prince is the dream of a blind mole living in a deep hole or a fat toad from a nearby swamp.

4.2548.

A woman can be compared to a Trojan horse, in the sense that when she gives birth to a child, everything in a man's life can change very dramatically.

4.2592.

If a man deprives a woman of her freedom, she will start looking for reasons to quarrel with him and leave.

4.2627.

First, a narcissistic woman loves herself, and then the meaning of her life becomes a child.

4.3013.

Husband-head, wife-neck. Where neck will turn, there husband

and looks. If the wife becomes the head, then the neck will be the husband and the woman will lose her power by becoming a puppet.

4.3141. As soon as a woman wants a child, she falls in love.

And Cupid the ugly and chubby. The image of Cupid reveals to us the true motives of love. All this action is necessary to the woman only for the sake of the baby as soon as she receives that desires, the man will be no longer necessary to her.

4.3206.

The woman takes offense at those whom she cannot enchant. It undermines her Ego's self-esteem.

4.3216.

Women like arrogant men, they inspire in them the hope that fear is a lie.

4.3490. Giveaway or a struggle for power.

A woman will fall in love with a man whom she cannot defeat while being sometimes capable of defeating him. Men love in a similar way. This is why truly durable relationships are about both of them constantly quarrelling, making up and winning in turns.

4.3505.

The man is hard and small, and the woman is huge and liquid. Huge egg as a whole absorbs a little sperm.

4.3560.

A woman loves only a warrior, but rather for fun. Female hero joyful. There is no greater joy for a woman than to belong to a hero.

4.3589.

Happiness is hardly possible for a man who runs after women. Women can not run, it leads to suffering and failure.

4.3591.

Women in the absence of men become men, but women do not like to be men. A woman would like to find a man so that she herself would not be a man.

4.3661.

A woman needs to admire her man to love. But better get used to it, so if a man will not grow, the woman quickly get used to it and stopped to admire, and lose sexual interest.

4.4157. Mistakes of men when dealing with women.

There are traits, certain properties of the male character, which on an intuitive level will tell a woman that a man is immature and not suitable for a relationship, after which a woman will AUTOMATICALLY feel disgusted and can stop loving such a man. Other things being equal, it is bad when a man complains, whines, scared, bad-mouthing other people, all unhappy, helpless about the philosophy of nihilism, suffering. Suspicion, jealousy and distrust speak of insecurity and weakness. You should defiantly believe the girl. Women are very timid and touchy, so scaring them with their anger and inadequacy is a bad idea. If a normal woman feels like a man is looking for mommy number two in her, she'll probably run away. The woman herself is very timid and she wants to be protected and saved from everything. She didn't need an immature, weak man unless her maternal instinct worked. On the other hand, if a child is born in such a relationship, the woman will turn this instinct on him, and from the man will begin to aggressively demand his masculine essence.

4.4158. Boasting.

It's about men's age-old habit of always boasting and sermonizing. On one hand, this annoys everyone and arouses contempt and, on the other hand, women love with their ears. For a woman to love a man, she has to admire how smart and strong he is. One should pay attention to what kind of woman she is. What can amaze her and what can annoy her. It is very dangerous to boast in front of women of high social status. The smarter a woman, the more sophisticated a peacock's beauty should be. The stupider a woman, the quicker she will believe a man's nonsense. All other things being equal, a man has to be very smart and sagacious if he wants to talk to a woman from the top league, i.e. a beautiful, smart and rich woman.

4.4159. How to build a relationship with a woman.

Actually, nothing. Building relationships is the task and meaning of women's lives, the task of men-to engage in personal self-improvement and creation of the world. A man whose purpose in life is to run after women or seek female love is an immature man, little suitable for a relationship. In General, in terms of relationships for men, the main thing to adhere to the ritual. Looking for signs of love and if these signs are not flows into the fear and go berserk. A frightened woman is a terrible person. Signs of love are necessary. A little, just 10-15 minutes a day, a couple of gentle words, a smiley face, ask how you are. The main thing is not to overdo it. Too much kills love. All these conversations for 2 hours a day should be strictly suppressed, 15 minutes and not a second more. A man has to work and is busy. A man who talks and doesn't do a damn thing is a defective man.

4.4160. How to become the kind of man women love.

First, you need sincerity and honesty. Honest people are strong people. A woman likes strong men. Honesty is strength. The second force is the mind. A man should read more, and not fairy tales, fiction and narrow literature on the specialty, and such types of literature as non-fiction, Economics, philosophy and psychology.

4.4161. Why a woman does not pay attention to her husband after the birth of a child.

After the birth of the child (and before that), the woman biologically concentrates all her attention on the child. To attract her sexual interest, a man should actively pay attention to the child and deal with it. After the birth of a child, a woman's sexual desire will depend very much on how the man treats the child.

4.4162. Why did the woman leave me?

There are four main factors why a woman loves a man. Accordingly, if none of them is not, then there is no reason for love and relationships. If a man does not deal with himself, immature and does not know how to love, the relationship with him is meaningless.

1. She admires the man. There are a number of factors for which he can be respected, for example: strength of mind, strength of spirit, striving for perfection, perfection of the body, the presence of his dreams and growth factors. Women admire strong and honest men. When a woman looks at a man, she sees him as her unborn child.

2. This man loves her. There are a number of criteria that determine whether a man loves a woman or not. For example, such criteria as trust, respect, kindness, generosity etc. a Loving man seeks to possess and dominate, but wants to care for and admire.

3. Biological availability factor. When body biology motivates a woman to want a child, she falls in love with the best available candidate.

4. A man should be Mature. Immature and weak man is not suitable for relationships. Women sense immature men by their indecision, aggressiveness, distrust, suspicion, suspiciousness,

insensitivity, depression, vileness and stupidity.

4.4163. Toxic woman. Which women should be avoided.

This is quite a complex and multifactorial question. In General terms, you can say that you need to see if this man is able to admire this woman. A woman can't love a man she thinks is beneath her. It is necessary to look closely at the woman's parents, her career. Materialistic and fixated on money women is also questionable partner.

4.4164. Why do I have a problem with women?

In short, women love honest, strong, intelligent and courageous men. Women love men who grow up and strive for perfection. You're probably not one of them.

5.1044.

The cause of female neurosis is male cowardice. A neurotic man is full of fears and does not grow, such a lack of growth and beauty in him plunges a woman into panic terror, because next to such a man she can not fulfill her destiny.

5.1052.

The manner of a woman to reveal to a man all the secrets of her bad Self has a deep meaning of the symbol of bread and salt. True beauty is flawed beauty, and a man who has fallen in love with his fantasy must now break it and fall in love with the real beauty of a real woman.

5.1312.

Every woman has her own demon.

5.1323.

A woman is not ready to give up her passion just like that.

5.1362.

Fear weakens a man, bisecting his personality, and most women, all these personalities 8, as the cat lives.

5.1717.

Women should be attracted, flowers attract butterflies and bees. Violence and aggression there will be extra. The man should encourage the beauty and power of the soul and body of a woman, not scare her.

5.1799.

Women are more honest than men in a contractual relationship with the big, but the small does not inspire them.

5.2252.

The sea, as a woman, is warm and gentle, and there is a storm and wind.

5.2438.

With age, women become harder and men softer. The level of the hormone testosterone in men falls, and menopause, on the contrary, strengthens the stability of the female psyche.

5.2443.

Women want a lot of sex from the man they love. Therefore, if a woman does not want sex from her man, love has passed and "wilted tomatoes".

5.2512.

If a female sees no code sequence of words and movements in the ritual dance of a male, she will take him to be the male of a different species and will not let him approach her for mating. A man should inspire and ravish a woman, otherwise this man is not of her species.

5.2544.

Women, producing the hormone oxytocin, form in men a social community of a single group, forcing them to love their own and not to love others. Oxytocin turns men into soldiers ants protecting their nest. This is one of the reasons why in Christianity priests were supposed to limit sex, because Christianity was an interstate religion, and women form in the soul of a man patriotism and love for the homeland and community.

5.2557. You want to go to the police?

Popular rumor and even me... they say that if you beat a woman and then beg for forgiveness, she will fall head over heels in love with you... (you can not only beat in the face, and words).

5.2612.

Empathy women and their willingness to look at yourself through the eyes of strangers due to the distrust on yourself, emotional instability and hormonal monstrous error of looking at the world from inside yourself. The female mind has difficulty controlling its body and needs external control and confirmation of the correctness of its actions.

5.2662.

They say there's nothing worse than an over-loved child, it's a lie, an over-loved woman is an order of magnitude worse than any child.

5.2937.

Oxytocin creates the addiction to the smell. The smell of each sexual partner is unique. Such programming creates a man addicted to sex with a partner.

5.2938.

Men love the hormone oxytocin, and women love the idea of motherhood.

5.2980.

Running after women, a man recovers excess energy and time, which he apparently has nowhere to go.

5.2989. Chronicle of the loser.

A man always serves its dream and if his dream-woman, then all his money and time this woman and inherited, and when love end, will remain this a man nor with than...

5.2999.

Women are almost always bored and they always favor men who have the ability to entertain and attract them.

5.3000.

Women love compliments, but don't like men, awkwardly and roughly of them wanting. A compliment is an art that you need to train and educate yourself.

5.3002.

Women love order, disorder drives women crazy.

5.3003.

Usually a woman expects even more from her husband than her mother does from her father...

5.3041.

Female (rarely male), when they felt a lack of attention and begins to fear that her love, provokes a strong scandal, offending and bringing a partner to the limit only to at the last second, stopping a partner from leaving, to prove to himself that once he quits, it means he likes her ...and, then, all is well.

5.3278.

The woman very useful for a man, that one with his eyes kills the fear in him and inspires on feats. Admiring female look-the source of the hero's strength, going to the feat.

5.3376.

Metaphor the Homeric Helen is an eternal reminder of what suffering can involve everyone and all the love of an idiot to the woman.

5.3383.

The easiest thing to admire is the one that delights you. Women, feeling their power over a man, willingly surrender to his power... However, this scheme works everywhere.

5.3418.

Service is flattery. When you love a man, you flatter him. Flattery is pleasant. Especially love the flattering dreams and women... everyone likes flattery, though.

5.3672. Nobody likes to be unnecessary.

Strong women are often lonely ...they don't want men, and men don't like to be unnecessary.

5.3689.

The female manner to adapt to all tastes and ideas of the man steel chains chains the man to it. Men are vain, finding a soul mate, they can not live without it.

5.4049.

Ocytocin is a thing whose absence causes stress and anxiety. By stimulating the production of this hormone in her man and children, a woman makes them feel anxiety and stress, when she has long been absent, and joyful calmness, when she is present.

5.4557.

A woman falls in love when she gives up, when she can't stand the onslaught. A man, on the contrary, loves until he surrenders.

5.4669.

Only another woman can protect a man from a woman. Other ways to protect ourselves against women we do not know.

5.4708.

First a woman says she wants nothing from a man but a child, then she wants nothing but money for that child.

5.4809.

The thesis from the Old Testament that Canaanites should be avoided when choosing a wife is related to idolatry and the Canaanite philosophy. A man falling in love with a woman begins to believe her and can easily convert to the faith of his wife. In a broad sense, a man should avoid women idolaters, otherwise they will sacrifice him to their idols. Such a woman will destroy the faith of a man, make him stupid and weak.

5.4957.

It is dangerous to love a pagan, she will fall in love with a man, make an idol of him, turn him into a demon, and demons, although strong, are doomed to suffer. And then the Pagan will give birth to a child and fall in love with him, and the demon will remain without love and will burn, and as a drug addict will plunge into an impassable narcotic withdrawal.

5.4962.

The state of passionate love in all women is described in the same way. Madly attracted to him and this feeling is in the chest, from the collarbone to the stomach. Feeling of heat, tightness and difficulty breathing. If the object of passion is not available, the state becomes unbearable and maddens with despair, pain and fear. However, many men feel the same.

5.4974.

Self-justification is a woman's hobby, no man is able to justify himself as much as even the most recent woman in this matter.

5.5068.

A woman can be led, but a woman cannot be commanded. A man can be command, but to wage his undesirable.

5.5069.

Problems with orgasm are either very cowardly women from fear, or very strong from contempt and pride.

5.5074.

Women do not like obsessive men, because obsession is a sign of immaturity and inability to love. Other signs of immaturity are suspicion and aggression. That's what stupid kids and teenagers do, but not Mature men.

5.5129.

Not woman and man are attracted to each other, but femininity and masculinity, weakness and strength, hardness and softness, lies and truth.

5.5131.

The essence of a woman's power is not to protect herself and the child, but to find those who will protect her.

5.5137.

Love woman to man is a woman's admiration of her man and the desire to immortalize it by creating a offspring. A woman wants to multiply what she likes.

5.5339.

Love makes men patient and women impatient.

5.5340.

The sight of a woman arouses a man's desire here and now. Thus, a woman by her appearance returns a man to reality, prompting him to take immediate action.

5.5519.

In modern times, women have achieved the power and power that is able to raise children without the participation of men. This situation is constrained by men's fear of the legal consequences of such relationships. The situation when a woman wants a child, and a man does not, can be considered as a sperm donation and accompanied by a legal contract, removing from the man financial and other obligations towards the child.

6.1063.

A woman demands his attention and his interest, his admiring gaze and tenderness... She should, but whether she should be given it is another matter.

6.1098.

A man's desire is a woman, a woman's desire is a child. A woman should understand that a man loves a child through his love for a woman. If a woman deprives a man of her love, she will jeopardize the love of the child, and therefore the entire energy supply system.

6.1099.

A woman who lives not by reason but by feeling wants a child. To get a child, she uses a man, seducing him with her passion. Having received the child, the woman directs her passion to the child, wanting his love and tying the same as before the man... And at this time, deprived of love, the man suffers greatly, experiencing narcotic withdrawal. In General, drug hunger binds him to this woman, but if a man is strong and perfect, he can run away or be led away by another woman.

6.1101. Everything is repeated in a circle.

The mechanics of female marriage can be divided into three parts. The first time she's getting married out of stupidity, second time, wanting the child and only in the third either because really falls in love with a man or...

6.1140.

From a woman's love can be many causes, mainly the desire for a child, the fear, the hunger, the desire to escape from parents, etc. to the satisfaction of his desire, the woman loses interest in men.

6.1352.

A woman always wants to admire and admire, it gives her integrity. Split personality brings pain and fear to a woman.

6.1354.

Women are passionate about love and admiration, and also overflowing with passion for those they love. Meanwhile, religion tells us that by creating idols and idols, we fall into hell.

6.1432.

A man should make sure that his wife does not fall in love with her child, otherwise he will lose both his wife and child. Love turns a woman into a drug addict, can save her work, household chores, Hobbies, sports, self-love.

6.1530. Avoid demons.

A man who has no other passions than love for his woman is a monstrous danger to a woman. Such love denies freedom and causes a lot of suffering.

6.1604. Man is for woman and leader, and servant.

6.1880.

Don't believe women who say you can't escape fate. It's women who don't choose what they love. Strong-minded men decide what to love. The strong in spirit control their love as they see fit, and choose their own destiny.

6.1881.

They say that women are the weaker sex, it's all because a woman does not choose what and whom to love, her nature decides everything for her.

6.1944.

The history of civilization is a love story... a love story of women for perfection and their children, who, having accepted this perfection with their mother's milk, built a new world.

6.1961.

For women, life is a game of relationships, and for men-a designer, where he collects from small details something whole.

6.1962.

Although the woman herself loves peace, but when a man falls into peace, she does not like it. And she starts to pull him and pull, so he did not relax.

6.1963.

A man forever wants to collect its designer, and woman wants relations ...and, if a man is too fond of his construction, the woman begins to get bored and provoke him to a relationship, for example, through scandals.

6.1982.

Women love relationships and are very bored when a man ignores them. Many men do not understand what a relationship is. Prompt ...it's different games, including role-playing.

6.2062. Biomechanical people.

A man collects perfection as a constructor, and a woman grows it as a plant... But most of all I like biomechanical systems.

6.2081.

Women do not like to be angry with them, they are willing to do much for the sake of not being angry with them.

6.2117.

Lack of sex breeds in a man irritation and aggression, and then keen desire to run away, which, if not realize, turns into apathy and indifference to wife. By the way the mistress in such a system even saves some relationships, because, fled to his mistress, the man removes cognitive dissonance and instead of indifference to his wife feels guilty in front of her.

6.2373.

A woman is the main temptation of a man. A man who can overcome a woman's temptation will gain incredible strength.

6.2485.

The woman is like water, it wins hard and soft rules, obeying. Not a stone to break the water, not fight. With tenderness holds his water, never by letting go.

6.2582. Freedom to first be sad and joyful tears.

A woman is afraid of negativity and anger for the same reason that water is afraid of hardness and fire. Faced with a hard hot anger, the water instantly boils and evaporates, so finding freedom. Freedom is joyful until the first rain.

6.2584. Water in a jug and children are the flowers of life.

Woman is naturally soft as water and life-bearing. Women love hard men because they give them shape, protecting them from fear, and allow, concentrating efforts, better to follow their goals and purpose.

6.2585.

Water can also be hard, and this hardness is called coldness and ice. When a man has no firmness and restraint, a woman is forced to turn to ice next to him. The cold woman is not able to generate life, but only kills it.

6.2799.

Women are very attentive to detail and love to look into faces. This, first, prevents them to see whole, and second, plunges their soul in eternal fear and anxiety.

6.2833. But they believe in feelings.

Men are very trusting and egocentric, and inclined to believe everything they are told, women in this respect much less believe the words.

6.2882.

Women are on average smarter than men. More than half of men are stupider than women, and the smaller half is smarter.

6.3187.

Women have a division of personality, each person loves independently and is not connected with each other.

6.3206.

A woman needs a man with a dream, such a man will not burn her with his neurotic love and insane harassment. With such a man, you can maintain a distance without being afraid to burn in the sun.

6.3214.

Women do not like negativity and are ready for any deception, just to avoid it. And women are very fond of templates and are ready for any deception to keep the script unchanged. Any change in the pattern is seen by them as a negative and unpleasant factor.

6.3312.

Female - liquid, male - solid. All actions of a woman are motivated by the actions of a man.

6.3316. Does a woman act differently?

A man can't just leave his woman, he has to suck the excuse out of his finger to make her look guilty, or he'll go mad with remorse.

6.3330.

More than anything, a woman should be afraid of herself.

6.3381.

Women are the weaker sex because they cannot resist deception, they are forever deceiving themselves and there is nothing they can do about it.

6.3396. Be careful to feed the women with gingerbread.

Women are afraid of gingerbread, because they know that it is cheese in a mousetrap. The wild fear of being in a cage causes cognitive dissonance in a woman, she feels anxiety and irritation. The subconscious is looking for any excuse to quarrel and run away, then somewhere alone the hellish suffering to cry from fear and pain.

6.3444. Rarely there anyway.

The weaker sex is called weak because that woman always reflects. Her behavior is usually a consequence of the behavior of men.

6.3646. Extremes kill love.

Love disappears if she did not pay attention or, conversely, to Deplete the passion. It is very important for a woman to maintain a man's attention to himself, but not to cross the line.

6.3676. Mindfulness is love.

Women love yoga and meditation... Yoga is involvement and concentration, i.e. love. Love is order. Women love love, order, yoga.

6.3823. The nature of women.

I have noticed that women, in order to get married (or break up a family), play very complex scenarios, and often do it quite unconsciously. That is, where she could be accused of a treacherous and cunning plan, it is not she who works, but her subconscious.

6.3827.

Men touch of jealousy invigorates them it like a moose during the rut, - fool.

6.3829.

Little that drives men crazy more than unobtrusive sexual innuendoes and circumstances.

6.3830.

If a woman sets herself the goal of dominating him, a man has no chance of escaping from a woman without the help of a psychologist.

6.3893.

Women despise low-spirited men and admire high. The former live by the baser instincts of the body, and the latter by the higher aims of the mind.

6.3918.

When a woman says that she lacks love, it means that she lacks signs of attention, she is given little attention and time.

6.3919.

The relationship between a man and a woman is a kind of game the goal of which is the struggle for power. Who loves, he is lost.

6.3945. She likes being a river.

Women love men who take the initiative in a relationship, like the solid banks of the river. It relieves a woman of guilt, the need to think and make decisions.

6.3946.

Women are formal and squeamish, which is very sensitive to the appearance of men. Women are irritated by untrimmed nails, dandruff, eczema, dirt, untidiness, loud voice, sharp perfume, sweat smell, unpleasant smell, dirty clothes and shoes, many do not like bristles and unshaven.

6.3948. The longer the better.

In the long-nosed tribe, it seemed to women that the longer the nose, the more sexually attractive the man. In a tribe of long-eared women love the ears. That is the nature of passion.

6.3964.

Women love empty men because the outer form is very important for women. In search of the ideal woman often looks at the outside. Therefore, men who have fallen victim to lust, spend 100% of their efforts on the outside, which makes them very empty inside.

6.3989.

Bitchiness and scandals woman attracts attention and makes

a man think about himself. The more he thinks about her and spends time on her, the more he falls in love and becomes addicted.

6.4170.

When a woman asks for attention, she asks for time... love and money.

6.4179.

In the past, women were not allowed into temples and shrines, guided by the fact that God is pure reason, and a woman is able to drive men crazy, and thus kill God in them. That is the meaning of the burqa.

6.4180. Forget that this is a woman.

If you are a man, then in negotiations with women consciously control whether a woman drives you crazy with her femininity. In the absence of reason, a man is not his own master.

6.4413.

Women fall in love with the type of men amiable but distant. Men fall in love with women like that. To love side was able to overcome alienation, it should start the siege.

6.4499.

The essence of the femme fatale is strength combined with stupidity. The power of beauty and the weakness of reason give rise to foolish desires, give rise to an eternally hungry monster.

6.4534.

The femme fatale, as a symbol of evil, must necessarily accompany the birth of genius, a symbol of good. The unity of the stupidity of evil and the genius of goodness make for the beauty, the God of this world.

6.4566.

Women do not like men who do not have dreams. The dream is sexy and it turns a woman on.

6.4581.

Women love men who have a place to grow and do not like those who have only a place to fall.

6.4618. Hoity toity.

A woman is doomed to love the best biologically worthy offer available to her. Available to her those men who paid attention to her or she on them. Biologically, a woman aspires to what grows or aspires to beauty and perfection. Women are encouraged by everything that in her opinion can grow. Women love those who love them. Women love those who are kind to them.

6.4619.

Women love ears, because they are very inspired by the plans associated with growth and movement.

6.4701.

A woman should have a love of beauty. Surrounding herself with beauty, a woman becomes more beautiful and so attracts rich men, because money should serve beauty, and men are slaves of female beauty.

6.4781.

Avoid women who prevent you from doing your job and bring closer those who help.

6.4868. Broken love is expensive.

A woman who leaves a man in love with her must understand that it will be a huge loss for him. A man will fall into the depths of vices, give up work and lose a lot of time and money.

6.4880. To love is to devote time.

A woman does not just pass 100% of her love to a child, but because no one really helps her, and she spends all her time with him. If her husband helped her, he would also get some time and love.

6.4975.

Women are so arranged that they must love beauty.

6.4976.

A woman is so made that, if it is time for children, she will fall in love with anyone who shares this desire or anything like growing and living.

6.4980.

A woman does not fall in love with a man, but with his ideas or the idea of him.

6.4984.

Women like strong men... the weakness of the weak is the food, so they say the way to a man's heart is through the stomach. Weakness is lust and the road to them lies through the bed. The strongest men serve ideas and to find the key to them, you need to share with them their ideas and goals. The stronger a man is, the more he delights women.

6.5082.

Women are therefore at the mercy of patterns and stereotypes that they protect them from sudden hormonal changes in the body. The lack of order is detrimental to the female mind and drives her crazy.

6.5137.

The man stopped growing intellectually. Abandoned his body. Not reads. He doesn't play sports. Of course, he no longer fits her ideal, she is disappointed and does not seek sex.

6.5153.

Fat girls like men because they are associated with pregnancy and so, hinting at reproduction, seem sexually attractive.

6.5191. Women like men-hunters.

A true hunter is persistent and persistent in the pursuit of his prey. If a woman started running away from him, he'd be on her tail.

6.5224. Holy harlot.

The image of the Holy harlot Magdalene is close and understandable to any woman who loves her children, but, having fallen out of love with her husband, lives with him, children only for the sake of. Sacrificing herself for the love of children, a woman as if sacrifices her soul and body.

6.5270.

A woman falls in love with the image of a man, her dream of him and his lies about himself. However, then the illusion breaks and the woman is overtaken by a strong disappointment that everything is a lie, and, in fact, he is much less than his vain dreams. The question is whether he grows to his idea of himself or only dreams.

6.5288.

You shouldn't argue with the woman you love, the longer the quarrel, the more expensive reconciliation will cost you.

6.5292.

The woman is always consumed with fear. To get rid of this fear, she needs a man who will love her. When a man loves her, she can control him. The feeling of power gives a woman strength and, killing her fears, fills the soul with joy. That is why the most terrible female fear is to remain without love and attention.

6.5318.

A man should be very careful when choosing a mother for his children. A neurotic woman is able to turn into hell not only her life, but also the lives of her children and her husband.

6.5330. How to find a rich man.

Does anyone want to teach me how to play tennis?

6.5336.

Offending the man, the woman draws his attention to himself, and he falls in love. But better to give him a story or pleasant emotions that it used to.

6.5337.

The image of the glass slipper in the fairy tale of Cinderella is a man's attempt to find a replacement for his ideal. However, the ideal illusory image is so far from real people that real women do not fit. The Prince runs from one woman to another, realizing with horror that this is not the case, and goes crazy for the escaped Cinderella.

6.5339.

If a man has gone too far with passion and killed in woman love, then should bury the murdered woman and find itself a new living. On the other hand, there is a good chance that the old love after a while from jealousy will rise from the dead, but that's why you zombies.

6.5342.

If a woman asked her husband to help, she searches for its location. It's kind of a reason to be friends. Not receiving such help, she loses interest in him and disappears. And it's usually for the best.

6.5343.

The woman in his power can not defeat their passion, especially if she starts to beat her and then call you back. Be wonderful presents to alternate whip. But you need a delicate balance, any imbalance breaks the system. An overabundance of one leads to a lack of the other and everything collapses into the abyss.

6.5347.

A woman's idea that it is better to be loved than loved leads to the fact that she herself does not love the one who runs after her, and is then forced to look for a third - a lover to run after him. They say that's why most men raise other people's children.

6.5358. Like kills like.

For a woman, love passion is a matter of biology and childbirth. Because the woman thinks, in fact, not about himself but about the genetics of the offspring, such passion to defeat the power of the mind is highly problematic.

6.5369.

Women love is important. Women seek attention. Love is attention, attention is time, time is energy, energy is money and matter.

6.5447.

A man should not swear and make a woman claim that she refuses him sex, but should be offended, upset and leave. However, a woman can do the same.

6.5467.

If a woman is rowdy, you need to feed her meat or porridge. In emergency cases, you can drink coffee and eat sweet.

6.5472.

A woman was in a good mood, her need to feed, walk and attend to it. Very much on the behavior of women affects her hormones and calm.

6.5473. Women calm, when everything corresponds to the order.

6.5474.

A woman loves when a man likes what she loves, for example, her children, her animals, her work, her appearance and things. And sad, if it is not happening.

6.5475.

Women are pleased when everything goes according to plan and corresponds to the order of things clear to her. Inconsistency with the plan cause it anxiety.

6.5485.

When a man overcomes a woman with manic neurotic love, giving 100%, a woman biologically very much wants to love him, but the mind says "do not".

6.5486.

Time and money are interchangeable. When a man spends his time or money on a woman, he falls in love with her, for love is attention measured in time.

6.5507. Self-knowledge.

By mind, many women mean the ability to understand herself, to understand herself. Therefore, a smart man is one who knows how to speak openly and clearly about his inner world.

6.5515.

It has been observed that a woman who does not like oral sex with her man does not really love him. Most likely, such a woman loves herself, maybe something else, but this man she only uses and nothing more. At least, about any unity or admiration of the man in such relations there is no speech.

6.5549. Softness tends to hardness.

The hardness of the man stands still, but it is worth the water to approach, trying to master him, his hot passion stone makes the water boil and, soaring to heaven, rejoice. So women love real men-restrained and firm in their hot passion.

6.5552.

Women in their passion want to admire what is growing, because men love to brag. The woman reproaches him - do not lie, but the body stretches.

6.5612.

A woman is the weaker sex because it is difficult for her to resist the devil's neurotic love, and if the devil loves her, she will not be able to resist him. It is also hard for a woman to resist the perfection of the devil. And yet the feeling that she gained the power of his love over the devil, gives it a heady joy of pride, so turning her into a slave of the devil.

6.5639.

A woman thinks that if she can control a man, then he loves her. Accordingly, if a man shows her that he is controlled, she will understand that he loves her and also fall in love with him.

6.5640. However dogs and cats she likes.

A woman likes to feel like a tamer of a wild beast, a pony also touches her for a while, but the power over sheep drives into boredom.

6.5641.

A woman likes the idea that she is courting someone, and that someone loves her like a dog, or warms her like a cat.

6.6022.

Women, just feeling the love, I want children, because children is their growth and fruiting, but immature men are cowardly, because they understand that if the blind lead the blind, all fall in the ditch. However, children and men generate a thirst for growth, because children need to feed, you need to earn more money.

6.6025.

Man daily activities absolutely necessary for three reasons. First, it is a good reason to take a shower every day. Second, it relieves stress, the source of all human suffering and disease. Thirdly, it is the subduing of the passions of the body and the key to the beauty of the body. A man with a beautiful strong body is always sexually attractive to women.

6.6130.

After the birth of a child, a woman risks falling so deeply in love with her child that she will be tormented by paranoid fears of everything. The reason is that the hypocrisy will make her afraid that something will happen to her and it will destroy the child. Such a mother is afraid of everything that threatens her and the child. Methods of struggle are those that need to break their love child to begin to trust other people, etc.

6.6367. Correct vector.

Either the man consciously grows and improves, or the subconscious of women leaves him without sex and his love. Women love those who grow from inferiority to perfection. Women love children, that's their feminine instinct. The main property of a good child is the presence of growth factors.

6.6368.

If a man is not able to offer a woman anything but pleasure and entertainment, he will not be able to be interesting to her for a long time. Vice is decay, and women love anything that grows and only when it grows. A woman needs a growth factor, otherwise she will become bored, and she will lose sexual interest.

6.6383.

The woman loves what grows, so if there is no movement, the woman is very quickly becoming bored, sad, and lost all sexual and other interest in life. If a man wishes to retain a woman's interest in him, he must change and grow as a child grows.

6.6410.

A young woman can love an old man only if he continues to grow.

6.6418.

Women like to provoke men to scandal when they are oppressed by relationships. Unconsciously and in a thousand and one ways they provoke a scandal.

6.6457. Honey, I'm tired today, and I have a really bad headache.

Idealists often men patients women who use disease or a million other excuses to curb their sexual desire of power.

6.6459. Headache and sex.

Women feel that too much sex love men, and refusal Angers. Therefore, in order not to cause conflict, they prefer to be ill forever. The male to maintain sexual interest of a woman to himself, should exercise restraint in requests for sex. She asks, but if she asked me to show passion. A man should be hot when water is poured into him, and without water it is foolish to bask.

6.6502.

Muse the one that can infect man and dreams to get a man to love yourself to fulfill them.

6.6523.

The victory of a man for the heart of a woman is his defeat, for now he, having lost his freedom, belongs to her.

6.6546.

The meaning of the parable of Delilah and Samson is that a man who has fallen into the passion of love loses his strength and becomes an easy victim of his enemies and vices. Delilah is a symbol of passion and service to all sins and idols.

6.6622.

A man who is not afraid to give everything for the love of his wife will get everything he wants.

7.1020.

A witch is a woman who is deaf to the voice of reason and lives solely at the mercy of her emotions, that is, the devil.

7.1183.

The woman is the first mate of the devil, who punishes man for his sins, weaknesses and vices. But a woman is also an angel of God, who rewards the righteous with his love. Love is the source of wonder.

7.1186.

A woman needs a man to control her fear. A strong man is a great medicine against any fears.

7.1293. Do you prefer being right or happy?

When the woman steps back, the man takes a step toward her. When a woman attacks, a man starts a war.

7.1318.

The main weakness of women's dependence on emotions and feelings.

7.1351.

Empathy is the main weapon of a woman, allowing her to intuitively feel what people around her want and, giving them this, get from them what she needs herself.

7.1365.

Empathy allows a woman to feel what a man wants from her and, by giving it to him, turn a happy victim into a drug addict and his faithful servant.

7.1375.

Women lie more often than men, they are forced to lie by empathy and fear. The woman feels very good companion and make him nice or not to hurt, likes to tell him what he wants to hear.

7.1377. Compassionate predator.

Clever women are well aware of what men want from them and, taking advantage of this, turn them into their servants.

7.1378.

Sweet woman is an empathic predator, in fact, a drug, a source of joy and pleasure, causing persistent addiction and affection in their victims.

7.1379. Tricky maneuver.

While children are small, it is better for a man to devote himself to war. Say, in search of energy for children females praying mantis eat their the males, so from sin away better work and not approach it too close and too often.

7.1382. Time mantis.

After the birth of a child, many women turn into female praying mantis. It is dangerous for a man to be near a female mantis during this period, because it can easily be eaten by sucking the energy out of it, sacrificing it to children.

7.1425.

In a relationship, a woman follows the spirit of a man, but for this she needs a strong-minded man. Weak men do not like women and are extremely aggressive to him, for only one thought that their joint child can be weak, very angry.

7.1463.

In solitude, a woman has a split personality, a source of eternal anxiety. When love comes, the split disappears and there is peace and wholeness... It's called happiness. When love dies, voices in the head and uncertainty returns.

7.1469. Dependence on external circumstances.

Bifurcation and reproduction of personality is a normal female state. With some it is one, others with another, the third, fourth tomorrow. And only love can make a woman whole.

7.1494.

Women think in images and live in images themselves.

7.1575. What to talk about with a woman.

Ask her about her childhood, her tastes, what she likes...

7.1634.

A man is one who serves his purpose. If your woman interferes with the achievement of your goals, part with her and find one that will inspire you. A normal woman is a Muse that inspires a man to feats in the name of serving his Purpose.

7.1635.

A woman is not a man's goal, she is the one who helps a man to follow his goal, inspiring and empowering.

7.1688. Psychosis.

Any emotions are very harmful to mentally ill people. It's like a house of cards, it is necessary to allow at least one emotion, all the others will immediately fall down and complete psychosis will begin.

7.1756. Woman's nature.

Women are full of fears. Fear is stress. The best ways to deal with stress is to communicate, chat, care about something or someone. Getting rid of stress, that is, fear, gives peace. Peace is joy.

7.1781. Happiness inspires.

It is vital for a woman to be happy, a happy woman is magnetic, she attracts a man and inspires him. If a woman can't inspire a man, she can't attract him.

7.1807. Women love donkeys.

Women like to turn men into donkeys, because the donkey is a good and necessary animal, very useful in the economy.

7.2061.

The instinct of creation and the instinct of destruction. Sex is a creative instinct. Women who love sex will be good mothers.

7.2182.

Princess on the pea is a very foolish woman, ready to use even the most frivolous pretext for the scandal.

7.2216.

I heard a story about a smart woman, who used to refuse her husband intimacy when he was complaining about his diseases. They say, this good man was known for his excellent health.

7.2534. Don't scare the woman.

A man should be afraid to inspire fear with his aggression and inadequacy to a woman. If a woman gets scared or realizes she can't calm or control him, she will leave and it will be extremely difficult to get her back. The woman runs away from fear.

7.2535. Women are extremely disliked by unreliable men who leave them.

A man not desirable stray from women, because he offended by. A man's resentment will pass quickly enough, but a woman's will not. Moreover, they say, women's resentment does not pass, it can go by the wayside, but no more.

7.2536. Inadequate men are scary.

Women are afraid of men they can't control. A man, if he does not want to lose his woman, needs to cultivate the idea of his controllability and adequacy.

7.2629. Prince in a mousetrap.

A woman is such a predator that you need to catch her desires. A woman, wanting to catch a man, looking for a stereotype and pattern, finding that madly rejoices, losing all vigilance.

7.2797.

Avoid women who are "bigger" than you. A woman should admire and rejoice in her man... otherwise she would eat him. The female mantis eating her male partner is much larger than him.

7.2808.

Women do not like it when someone is angry with them. Anger is an unfinished murder, an attempted murder. Women are afraid when someone wants to kill them and from fear try, if they can, to run.

7.2850. Better get busy.

It happens that a woman is disappointed in a man, ceasing to see a man in him. In her eyes, such a man loses his masculinity, strength and sexual attractiveness. In such a situation, a man needs to regain masculinity, a keen mind, take up work, begin to show male virtues. On the contrary, such actions as nagging, talkativeness, constant shaking, heartbreaking, licking, hugging and other slobbery tendernesses will have the exact opposite effect and will enrage a woman extremely.

7.2852.

Swearing, a man should not leave, leaving his woman alone. Women do not like to be left alone with their fears and regard this behavior of a man as a betrayal.

7.2860.

Female irrationalism is very useful to her in the fight against men. Man, guided by rationalism, assumes that the woman belongs to him, that he is her master, that she will not run away... And this rational reasoning turns him into a monster. But the woman, using irrational arguments, says he is not... all your conclusions about good and bright-nonsense, you are bad, and I will run away from you. This state of Affairs allows a woman to keep a man in vivacity, attention and fear of losing a woman.

7.2885. The junk man.

A woman is very afraid of her fears and needs a man to protect her from them. When you swear, it is dangerous to leave a woman alone, because she can guess that fear can be overcome without a man. Which meant she wouldn't need the man anymore.

7.2947.

Your problem is your passion. Passion makes you afraid. You're too afraid of losing the object of your passion. But your love she as woman, and women not like fear and not like cowardly men.

7.3132.

A woman who is interested in a man wants to see that other women are interested in him. However, the same applies to men.

7.3262.

For a woman to submit to a man, he must first hurt her female pride. In response, she will try to test the strength of the man and hurt his mind. If a man's mind is strong, a woman will admire him and fall in love.

7.3263.

Women always speak in riddles, in another way they, apparently, can not. A woman is terribly lonely because no one understands her mysteries. A woman will automatically love the man who will understand her mysteries and understand them.

7.3264. How to win the heart of a rebellious Queen?

The story Of the Queen of Sheba and king Solomon is a love story that teaches us the relationship of man and woman.

7.3266. Inspiring hope.

When we first met through a letter (rumors) Solomon impressed the Queen of Sheba boasting. She then asked her advisers and servants if they knew anything about the man. Everyone said they didn't know anything about him and maybe he was a crook. Sheba, as befits a true woman, did not believe anyone and decided to check everything herself. Why did you go to hell in the middle of nowhere?

7.3267. Why would the Queen of Sheba to king Solomon.

Why of Sheba went to Solomon? What attracted her? What was her ulterior motive? Why so far? Why did Sheba not have a husband and children? The fact is, Sheba had everything and she was smart and strong, there was no one higher than her. The problem is that a woman can't love someone below her, someone she doesn't admire. However, a woman really needs a child. A child is a woman's true love. A woman can not risk a child, choosing a bad male, she needs the most worthy of all possible, preferably stronger and smarter than herself. A woman needs a man whose power she is ready to recognize.

7.3268. The four puzzles.

When in the glass pavilion of honesty Solomon lowered Sheba's self-esteem by criticizing her hairy legs, Sheba also decided to show openness and honesty by proving to Solomon that he was a fool. To do this, Sheba demanded that he answer three riddles to test his mind. However, when he answered 3 riddles, it's for a reference check asked him a Fourth mystery. The fourth riddle was not only a control, but it also served as a self-justification for hairy legs, for all the women refused to lift the hem in shame. By this Sheba meant that under the dresses all women are the same and Solomon must admit that she has normal legs. Solomon, by his wisdom, showed that he knew this also.

7.3485.

It is vital for a woman to find a companion with whom she can chat, and he would listen to her. Otherwise, she is at great risk of falling into depression with all the sad consequences of this case.

7.3570. Love your wife for your children.

The symbol of Medea in the Greek tragedy is that a man should not drive his woman crazy, because the victims here will be children.

7.3584. You'd think men didn't need to.

Women need constant approval of their actions, it gives them confidence.

7.3651.

For a woman, the fact that a man forgives her her whims and psychoses is proof of his love.

7.4123.

Of course, a woman does not want to say openly what she wants, but she is quite transparent and clearly hints about it.

7.4338.

Women have great authority over men. If a woman settles in your head, it will be catastrophically difficult to expel it from there. I suggest you should become a monk and avoid women. If you do not manage that, what can I do? Live and suffer.

7.4452. Remorse is unnecessary.

Try to avoid contact games from the category of "I am vulnerable", "am I so easily hurt", etc. That men that women are extremely unbearable in this role and not to offend them. On the other hand, you can ignore their grievances altogether. Such people are always offended at everyone and, first of all, at themselves.

7.4484.

A woman wants to be desired by everyone she sees as a man with a capital letter. Men with a small letter woman is not very interested, which is why men should pay special attention to personal growth.

7.4485.

Women often run away, but only to attract attention. But you don't have to disappoint her, you have to play along.

7.4493.

If a woman is hysterical, then she expects a man to display masculine qualities, for example, money. By the way, money is a very important male quality. A man without money looks very doubtful. Although, of course, he can and compensate for money in other their virtues.

7.4494.

A woman likes men who fit her ideas about a real man. Where do such ideas come from? "It's mostly jealousy. A woman is pleased to be proud of having such a man, who can be proud, so that the surrounding women envied and also wanted this.

7.4495.

Important properties of a man that he liked a woman. It is desirable for him to fall into the male stereotype prevalent in the region. A man should be different from a woman. If a man is different from other men in the direction of femininity and weakness, the woman will lose sexual interest in him

7.4497.

A real man is a woman's fantasy. But if the man gets at least partially in this image, he will become the man of her dreams.

7.4498.

Ordinary women's desire to cause the desire. A woman wants a man to want everything himself, not so that she told him. Flowers he should give himself, not when she requests. A woman wants the desire to come from him and if it does not, she will provoke him with hysteria, jealousy, running away, etc.

7.4499.

A man accustomed to obey orders and the woman, of course, it would be necessary to use it. The man waits for demands and instructions, but the woman is interested in his desires. She wants him to want what she wants and guess what she wants. The source of women's desires-stereotypes and templates, books and movies, friends, sisters, mom and parent family. The man in this situation saves that in principle if to think, desires at the woman not so much. Of course, if desire to perform small, grow large.

7.4502.

Strong women like to engage in phallic struggle with weak men to dominate them, to increase their self-esteem.

7.4504.

Women lose sexual interest in men deprived of phallic dignity. That is, to such men who have nothing to brag about and who can not be proud of.

7.4512. Unlucky Muse.

A woman should arouse a man's desire. The desire to love, create, live, learn, work... This is the woman we call the Muse. If Muse fails to inspire a man to desire, it is commonly called hysterical.

7.4551. The man of her dreams.

If the girl did not have a father, her expectations about men will be perfect and not softened by reality. Such a girl will expect from men what she was expecting from his mother, plus some ideal and illusory images created by her mother, books, friends, movies, etc. the Man of her dreams is a kind of an idealized collective image of men mom and dad in one person. Such a girl will be very difficult to take the image of a real man, very far from ideal.

7.4767.

When a woman loses the ability to inspire her man, she begins to scold and abuse him. Fear and discontent man, or corrected, or runs away. Running away, he can find a new Muse. Left, will find strength within yourself. Both are for the best.

7.4970.

If a woman is disappointed in her man, she will find a reason to quarrel with him, and the reason will be any, even sucked out of the finger. To fight with the reason sucked out of a finger is silly, find the real reasons and kill them.

7.4993.

It is very important for a woman to feel support, reliability and security on the part of her man.

7.4998.

For women there often isn't enough intensity in relationship, and they start seek for pretext for scandals and conflicts. Gentleness and obedience of men make women bored.

7.4999.

Few women are able to forgive a man if he begins to play a female role or show female emotions. Such a man will lose in the eyes of women respect and she will lose to him sexual interest.

7.5113.

A man who builds a relationship with a neurotic woman should not bring her too close to him, should not allow her to serve and please him beyond measure. Keep your distance. The time and attention given to such a woman should be strictly controlled. The neurotic woman knows no sense of proportion, and if she is not restrained, she will burn everything and everything with her love. An additional bonus from this behavior will be crazy unquenchable love and passion on the part of women.

7.5275.

The image of the sleeping beauty is an image of a woman, wandering in a delusive world while waiting for the prince of her dream.

7.5276.

Metaphorically, every woman is a sleeping Princess waiting for a Prince to come to awaken her to life with his kiss. On their own such a woman to live not can.

7.5319.

Do you know why women are more like darkness and men are more like light? Because men love with their eyes and for love they need light. And women love with their ears, and in the darkness they are satisfied.

7.5377.

A woman can be compared to the earth. A man with a peasant who looks after her, plants and harvests. Land is expensive, it needs to be cared for and it needs to be protected. Land is home, food, children.

7.5499.

If a man can deny a beautiful woman sex, that's what I call power of mind and spirit, only an enlightened person can resist such temptation. It's like enduring the temptations of the devil himself.

7.5523.

A woman, if she loves her man, gives him all her strength and energy.

7.5710.

The neurotic woman is very specific. When the biological clock gives the signal that she needs a child, she is overcome by anxiety and thirst for love. Finding the first more or less available male, she pounces on him with all the fury of 100% love, causing a narcotic love addiction. All this is perceived as crazy love. If everything turns out and manages to get pregnant, the woman loses interest in the male and switches all 100% of her love to the child, and the man falls into a narcotic withdrawal and becomes even more attached to the woman, constantly demanding love from her and receiving it drop by drop. Thus, the value of this woman is greatly increased in the eyes of the addict and he, although suffering, but serves her. The woman herself is no longer interested in this man. The child, receiving 100% of love, grows up defective and extremely neurotic personality, full of sins and vices. In General, everyone is unhappy, like the neurotics and addicts.

7.5920.

A neurotic woman seeks a master over whom she can dominate.

7.5934. Lies.

Women lie very sincerely in the sense that they consider their lies fair and absolutely necessary guarantor of harmony and good. Women's lies and hypocrisy is like minus multiplied by minus to plus was born.

7.5937.

When they say that a woman loves with her ears-it means that she greatly exaggerates the meaning of what she heard.

7.5945.

When a woman says she doesn't understand, it means she doesn't approve and she doesn't like it. If a woman likes something and approves of it, she sees that she understands it.

7.5946.

A woman should speak softly and gently, because in her understanding the truth - it is soft and gentle, but a lie is rude and aggressive.

7.6387.

A man who agrees to live with his wife's relatives is called a fool. However, the one who lives with her, too far gone from the first.

7.6492.

Women love smart men because the man carries the seed and the seed, and the mother is a woman, the seed takes and raises it. Therefore, a woman is very happy when her man has a rational grain in his head.

7.7031.

A woman always suffers. Somebody told her a child can save her from suffering. It's partly true, but it's when she doesn't abuse remedies.

7.7077.

Be careful, people, especially woman, are incredibly dubious.

7.7117.

The one who complacently waits for destiny is a quiet sort. Waiting for destiny is like a man waiting for a beauty to come to him and say – «Be my husband».

7.7218.

If a woman doesn't want to have sex with a man, therefore he doesn't make her admire him. He Is a weak, silly one...and she doesn't want to belong him at all. A woman wants to give herself to worthy one, and she doesn't get off on that's why mendacious and cunning men are extremely keen on lying and bragging.

7.7219.

On the one hand, a narcissistic woman is promiscuous in love, because she does not care who loves her, as long as she is loved. On the other hand, her conceit is very demanding and whispers to her that not everyone is worthy to love her. Again, because to pay for the love the lady wants, the sensible people run from it like the vampire.

7.7262.

It's very dangerous for a man to have sex with unknown and un-authorized women . This situation is potentially fraught with huge problems.

7.7433.

If people, especially women, don't like the way you talk, they don't care what you say, they just don't hear you and are totally focused on their "don't like"feeling. So try not to push and not to show aggression, and calmly and without tension tell some-thing. Like play, and the listener will let the viewer into the movie. The listener should listen and watch you, observing the mystery of how you talk to God.

7.7535. A multi-person person..

A classic woman has more than a split personality, she has a multi-personality, because for each of her significant contacts or situations, she creates her own new personality. One person for her husband, another for children, the third and fourth for work and the boss, the fifth for lovers (for each his own), the sixth, etc. for girlfriends.

7.7616.

A clever man will always be reserved and friendly with a woman, otherwise she will eat him or run away.

8.1117.

It's only love that can win the triumph over evil. Human evil na-ture is the direct consequence of need for love. They really lack love and it makes them evil.

8.1118.

She's always so different with different people. And certainly, she really needs a man who got something that she doesn't - stability and persistence.

8.1121. Love and snakes.

Son, if you found a woman, it's necessary to love her. A woman who doesn't feel loved, soon turns into a vampire or a snake. Trust me, a hissing snake in bed is quite a strange type of pleasure.

8.1122. Empathy.

Yes it's true that a woman is a reflection of her man in many ways. If a man thinks that his woman is a monster, it's just his own reflection or the result of his weakness.

As for the weakness. The thing is that a woman always reflects the strongest man known to her. Thus, if a man is weak he will face the personality of her parents, bosses or any other people including even fictitious characters (and it's especially offensive if a woman worships the personality of her lover).

A normal man should be strong and loving with his woman. This way he will get her reflected amplified love. However, even if he simply stays strong enough to play the role of the dominant partner, everything will be great.

8.1123.

A woman's dominant personality greatly depends on external circumstances. Parents, her man or bosses have a really bad influence on her state of being herself.

By the way, it doesn't mean that she often needs to be herself. A real person who once gets out to see the world, can evoke many questions.

8.1124.

Women are really very different, there is a great majority of HERSELF even inside her own self.

8.1126.

A very important trait of female personality connected with the conditions of survival and existence, is the tendency to adapt to particular situations.

A woman can be very different with different people depending on different situations. It may seem that there are many different personalities living within a woman. All these personalities are totally real and sincere, almost equal. The dominance of a particular personality depends on external circumstances and people around.

By the way, that's why many people like movies about split personality and multiple personality disorder. Soulmates, so to speak.

And that's why women are so sincere at lying. In essence, they don't even lie as from the point of view of the dominant personality they always tell the truth.

Taking into account the inner multiplicity that should be somehow compensated with something, there's barely anything in this world that women can appreciate more than stability, and barely anything more scary than instability.

8.1148.

Feminism is a direct consequence of the absence of available nice men for reproduction around a woman.

8.1177. The essence of a woman.

A woman is an accumulator and energy amplifier that draws energy from everywhere and gives it those people she loves (children, husband etc). It's possible to see a beloved (loving) woman as a great source of energy and good luck. Indeed, a woman may take a lot out of her owner, but as an energy amplifier she will give more energy back if she is properly treated. The more perfect and unique a woman is, the greater power she has.

8.1184.

To hell with freedom.

Women's craving for freedom and dislike for others' attempts to change them, can be easily explained by the fact that at some biological level a woman needs to choose the best of all available males. While males are persistent, fresh and disturb the process of choice. What if someone wrong will be chosen... Of course, it's necessary to put males on heels.

And there are two variants here. The first one is when a female finds the right male and chooses him... This way she will give up herself and forget all her other desires. The second variant is when some male will be so persistent at winning her heart that her soul will switch on the realization how precious she is for such an admirer and how ready he is to do many things for her. It's a good sign. The next moment protection will switch off and love will happen.

A loved person is allowed to do anything.

And the system of protection is important as a filter for the unnecessary.

8.1199.

Don't criticize women for aggression, feminism, impudence, love of freedom and other stuff like that as all those qualities of female soul were given by nature so that every woman would wait for the right man whose reproduction fits the necessities of human evolution. In other words, it's necessary for every woman to find true love and any mistakes about it are really unfavorable.

8.1200.

Feminism is not a matter of female self-identity, but rather a matter of the mind degradation of males. There are very few men who deserve love and it's really sad.

8.1240. A slipper.

A classical female fantasy on the subject of Cinderella is interesting with the fact that the Prince remembered her legs only.

8.1241.

Bluebeard is a sin of curiosity.
The Golden Fish is a sin of greed.

Cinderella is a very refined satire that reveals the essence of female desires, transience of opportunities and psychology of princes who fall for nice legs.
Frog Princess reveals how female nature greatly depends on circumstances.
Snake Gorynych is a collective character.
Koschei the Immortal is a proof that money doesn't buy happiness.
A Wishmaster, a genie in the bottle, free cheese - all of them should not be touched or released.

8.1254.

Female hypochondria is the state when her soul feels like flying but her hands don't feel like taking a broom.

8.1301.

Female self-sufficiency is quite harmful for personal life. A man feels useless next to an independent woman. And it hurts to realize a woman can do without you.

8.1308.

When a woman is her man's right hand and his comrade-in-arms, she will be really appreciated and seen as indispensible to life. How would you live without the right hand? It's terrible even to imagine it.

But if a woman got on her man's neck and let herself be a burden, it will be difficult for this man to carry her especially while going up the hill. There will be only one thought in his head- whether he should leave her.

8.1311.

A woman should be the right hand but not the third leg.

8.1312.

In consideration with a man, a woman should be compared with a cap from a toothpaste tube... Her mission is not to let him flow in thoughts uselessly.

8.1317.

A girl who is a real smart cookie can always pretend silly in order to make a boy get closer and then swallow him insidiously.

8.1327.

If you want something, don't give up until you get it. Desires are like women who like persistent admirers.

8.1358. Predestination.

A woman should use care, tenderness and sex to inspire her man into deeds and feats. She should be his muse and source of energy.

8.163.2.

A thousand of my faces is a function of mood.

8.1748.

Women are the evolution driver, choosing the best men, they move the civilization forward.

8.1753.

A man who treats his woman badly, commits a heavy sin that will make his things get in a degraded condition. Spending time and money on women makes karma better and brings good luck that will bring even more money than it was spent.

8.1754.

The amount of energy (money) that a man gets, depends on his women. This energy is not meant for him. His women who use him as a tool, get energy for fulfilling their goals. In essence, a Muse is the one who makes a man work.

The role of the muse can be performed by some goals that a man pursues. But a woman is better in it. The more beautiful and perfect a woman is, the more energy she is meant to get.

8.1760.

It's always the strongest/smartest/richest men who get the most beautiful women.

8.1761.

Beautiful women should be protected, it takes great power to have them. Perhaps, that's why many men feel weak and scared of beautiful women.

8.1837.

According to the idea of this world's existence, a beautiful woman is supposed to be given a beautiful house, a beautiful car and a husband or a father who would provide her with it.

8.2134. A goddess.

Fortune, destiny, dream - they are all women and thus, it's necessary to treat them like women. They may be picky and beautiful, may not love you back or may get on your neck, but still... you should love them, be patient and persistent, and sometimes even strict. And remember that women like people of actions, persistent and strong ones. And of course women like to be worshiped.

P.S. An important moment. There are many strategies of dealing with the fair sex and if they're used properly they will work. It's important to show imagination, a pretty woman should not be bored in your presence. Your presence should be nice for her body and soul.

8.2155.

Women don't get words, they definitely need to feel everything.

8.2258. Mental hermaphrodites.

"A man in a skirt" and "a woman in pants" are the types of mental hermaphrodism rather than sexual equality. And clothes have nothing to do with it- it's rather a matter of view of life.

8.2481. If a woman likes something it's a good sign.

8.2578.

More beautiful women prefer to worship the devil. Ideological ones like angels. But it's not that important. Especially because, in essence, there are no particular differences between angels and demons, people are the same but their work differs.

8.2627. And now apples turn her nauseous.

I think that Eve ate more than one apple of knowledge, at least a bucket of them.

8.2644. Mammoth hunters.

Women are useful in every way but not in mammoth hunting.

8.2792.

Alcohol takes off masks and shows us the real person and it's known that the real person wants sex the most, so many women are afraid of drinking fearing their desires.

8.2835.

A woman can be Happiness and Unhappiness, but it depends only on you.

8.2885.

A man really depends on his women as they inspire him into war. A warrior should avoid women who don't inspire into death.

8.2897.

Television and the internet give a false sense that there are many beautiful women.

8.2899.

And do you know why prince evaluated Cinderella from feet to top? Legs, hips, breasts... are the most powerful female weapons while a pretty face is unfortunately, not given to every woman. If men appreciated faces first, then mankind would probably die out. However, I always look at faces first. Perhaps I'm a fool who doesn't have an eye for beautiful women.

8.2901.

It's not that she liked prince, she just wanted to be a princess.

8.3083.

A single woman looks sexually attractive when as a hunter you feel that you can catch her.

8.3087.

A woman with an assault rifle is sexually attractive... she evokes an acute desire to conquer her.

8.3330.

Female brain is a multicore device where all calculations are chaotic and not dependent on each other.

8.3558. A perspective woman.

I noticed that a woman who once chose the right man for herself, keeps her youth and beauty for a longer time. It happens because beautiful women are meant for the right men...

And it's also a matter of genetics as they found each other by smell, their genes are really different and their children are wonderful. They are useful individuals from the point of view of reproduction, so nature itself takes care of them and keeps them young.

8.3559. A secret of youth.

A woman's youth and beauty are kept by the perspectives of reproduction. If a woman's partner is perfect from the reproduction perspective, then nature will take care of this woman in hope to get as many children from her as possible. Such woman will keep her beauty, youth and health for much longer time than it's usual.

A few more things that help to keep beauty and youth, include healthy food, coldness, harmonious contrasting alternation of emotions like positive/negative ones, beautiful goals in life, interesting work, beautiful clothes and things around, physical activity, cosmetic medicine, endocrinology.

8.3588.

The more differences there are between the DNA of a woman and that of her partner,the better. The DNA of her partner gets into her body to keep her youth and health. Sex with such a partner is nice, his smell is arousing and children from such partner will be more genetically perspective and healthy. It's possible to recognize such partner by his smell.

8.3628.

The more your woman loves you and thus, the better her mood is, the better your state of things, including financial ones, will be. A happy loved woman is a source of energy and good luck.

8.3635. Women often mix love and pity.

8.3774. A successful man.

A woman's desires make a man better... A man has to work and think more and it makes him more noble. Besides, resisting the never ending female desires, he trains his Will and as is known, Will is the base of any success.

8.3788.

Girls and boys are still full of illusions about each other, while adult men and women are already well aware of the monstrous nature of each other. And it's right as monsters should love monsters and there's no need to grimace hypocritically and deny the obvious.

8.3900.

A beautiful woman should be expensive. If you want to possess her, you should be able not only to buy her but also protect her. A beautiful woman is of high value and they will always try to steal her.

8.3931.

A woman is an energy storage that supplies those she loves.

8.3932.

A beautiful woman can be compared to a flower that grows in the sun and consumes its energy and later gives it to the ones she loves.

8.3958. A subtle hint with a tint of light vulgarity.

A woman in the man's eyes is a source energy and vice versa. It resembles the electrical generator operation when inside a magnetic coil there rotates a rotating element and produces electricity.

8.4012.

A man's betrayal of a woman is not when he has a one-night stand with another woman and not when he says something in his temper... A betrayal is when he finally refuses to care and protect her.

8.4016. She who inspires into deeds.

The meaning of a woman's life is to be a muse.

8.4026.

The essence of intellectual symbiosis between a man and a woman is that men are better at seeing the whole, while women notice more details.

8.4081.

Men really appreciate women who are able to forgive their sins. But over-principled women are single, as a rule.

8.4111.

The reason for women's neverending resentment over family life is trivial - they read many contrived fantasies in female literature and then try to put them into practice.

8.4112.

It's sex that a man wants from a woman most of all, while a woman wants anything else from a man.

8.4116. Beware of women. A woman is a source of pain.

When being a source of pain, a woman is potentially very dangerous.

8.4151.

A man should never marry a woman who is not philosophical enough to forgive his fits of anger and other faults.

8.4162. The power of love.

Any woman, once she becomes a Muse, is able to turn the man she loves into a Hero... Heroes are all mighty, they can control time, energy, money and good luck...

Heroes are the lords of the world and
Muses are the lords of the Heroes...

8.4169.

It's necessary to give emotions to a woman, even in the form of flowers.

8.4216. Invaluable.

The more a man is ready to pay for a woman, the more he likes her... And he's ready to give anything for his beloved woman.

8.4220.

It's necessary to forgive a woman all her stupid actions, otherwise she may get offended and leave... and it will be more expensive than just forgiving her.

8.4223.

A marriage between a man and a woman of the same age is a marriage of unequals. Girls who once learn to feel, become women at about 20, while boys become men who are able to think in their early thirties (at best).

8.4301.

Fifty shades of grey... a classical plot of "Cinderella" dished up like sadomaso, that fulfils a woman's desire to find a man stronger than she is so that to forget her fears with him.

8.4302.

Women always suffer from pain and fears. All their life is about escaping fears and pain, and it's their happiness. A woman needs a man who can protect her from her own fears.

Generally, there are many ways for a woman to escape fears, pain and suffering... it involves children, men, work, some sectarian clubs, yoga classes etc.

8.4306. A woman is, expenses in the first place.

8.4313.

Taking into account the power of women over men, the only thing that stops women from seizing the reins of the world is that they hate each other.

8.4316.

A smart man and a smart woman will barely get on well together, they will have a neverending conflict about who should think for whom...

8.4317. Wonderful stupidity.

Stupidity can make people wonder, and wondering is a source of energy... Thus, wonderfully stupid women produce a much stronger impression on men than smart ones do. Smart women evoke the alarm of doubts whether it's possible to conquer them...

8.4318.

A smart woman always tries to seem slightly stupid, so that not to cause unnecessary arguments.

8.4319.

Because of feminism, modern women have to work for some unknown people, while television educates children.

8.4321.

It's always a man whom a woman blames for everything.

8.4322.

Women understand little of things but feel everything at once.

8.4323.

A woman who is unable to be eternally forgiving with her man, is doomed to be single.

8.4324.

When I see a terribly beautiful woman, I become terribly worried about my purse.

8.4325.

It's women's limitless desires that created this world by means of male hands.

8.4326.

The more a woman wants, the more a man has to work... The more beautiful your woman are, the more you'll have to work.

8.4331. Motivation for personal growth.

A beautiful woman (the one you love). A beautiful woman is a drug and once you get addicted to her, you'll have to court her and serve her, fulfilling her wishes. But wishes become bigger, after fulfilling some wishes soon there will be other ones and bigger ones.

And you'll have to work more, becoming more perfect and gaining personal growth so that to earn enough money for sating the appetites of your ever hungry muse.

8.4332. The reverse.

From Muse can benefit and motivation, both directly and Vice versa. When Muse with you-she source of energy and inspiration, and when you its gonna lose ... your pain will be so great that to stop it you will have to work and create endlessly in an inglorious attempt to escape from the pain...

8.4342.

Women can be beautiful and useful, the latter ones are better.

8.4350.

Love demands something in common, for example both partners can love herself only.

8.4357.

Women can be useful and can be drugs.

8.4359.

Choose the more beautiful of two evils. Of two evils, choose the one you like more.

8.4363. Flattery is water.

Men emaciate without flatter and women wither without it.

8.4365. Work for creators.

Beautiful women love beautiful things and that's why God the Creator loves them and those who pay for them.

8.4370.

Beautiful women are a great motivation for a man to earn more.

8.4378.

Why does a man have to forgive a woman all the time? May she forgive her own self.

8.4386.

When dying, love turns into hate and disgust. She feels disgust and he feels hate. This is their reaction to pain.

8.4429. A lying mirror.

It's not a woman who gets reflected in a mirror but it's a mirror that reflects in a woman. A mirror often lies to its owners, but only because they only see what they want to.

8.4453. Even though perhaps I get something mixed up.

Many women have a talent to choose the biggest stupidity of all possible ones... Men are more modest in this way and the size doesn't mean much for them.

8.4456. However...

This world is ruled by men, and men are ruled by women, while women are ruled by their fitness or yoga instructors, cosmetologists, female books writers, internet-reads, tv, mothers and friends.
... I even start to feel somehow scared...

8.4457.

Feminists are very aggressive, gentlemen don't behave this way.

8.4459.

As a man, I support feminism and approve of equality. In everything... especially in expenses... And I'm terribly angry as not a single woman has ever given me flowers or asked me out to some restaurant... And by the way, I really want to be courted, kept, given presents and made love with for all those things...

8.4474.

Women resemble cars: Bentley, Mercedes, Peugeot, scooter, pedal cycle... The more beautiful a woman is, the more expensive and impractical she is... A beautiful car is love, passion... it's emotions...

8.4477.

A beautiful expensive woman is better than an unattractive cheap one. But it's even better when a woman is useful... Useful women are obviously more useful than any other types of women...

8.4481. Love is blind.

All women are beautiful by touch...

8.4501.

It's very nice to be a muse and inspire someone.

8.4505.

It's better agree with a woman... or disagree- depending on what she would like to hear more...

8.4509.

Beautiful women are terribly expensive. It's fear for their purses that makes men scared of them.

8.4513. Taming of an animal.

There's only one thing that a woman should know about a man: a man is ready to forgive a woman anything on the condition that she satisfies his sexual appetite and lets him lie and be boastful...

8.4522.

When I look at some beautiful woman I really want to work. I mean, beautiful women are an expensive luxury that demands great expenses.

8.4527.

A woman is the type of fish that on her own looks for a hook that they would catch her on.

8.4546.

A woman resembles a cat: she also needs to be fed and petted. But cats are different too: some of them are useful mouse catchers while others are simply fancy.

8.4552.

Muse is the beauty that raises the Spirit of Genius.

8.4553.

I think I've already said that it seems that angels are women and demons are men... Though sometimes it's vice versa.

8.4566. A talk with a dealer about Love.

I don't want to deal with you and waste my time and money on you until I get the proof that you have love.

8.4567. An Angel.

An innocent but endlessly naughty girl, isn't it the embodiment of perfection for a man?

8.4569.

Women rarely hate anyone, they mostly feel disgust that makes them run away. While real men rarely run away from anyone and that's why prefer to hate and thus, to attack.

8.4571. Devotion comes first.

Never leave a devoted woman for a pretty one. The same for business: a devoted colleague is more valuable than any others no matter how perfect or highly-qualified they can be. A devoted person is the best one that cannot be replaced by anyone better.

8.4578. Free from men.

The essence of sectarians' work on female mind is that they try to provide a woman with power to live without a man, giving substitute like yoga, fitness and work... so that a woman would not be controlled by a man but would be ruled by her Guru or Trainer.

8.4579. Cheating.

For women fitness, jogging and yoga are some kind of substitutes for sex, with all strange consequences it may involve.

8.4583.

They say that a woman should belong to a man... Perhaps, it's true. Renting is less expensive, but those who rent somehow refuse to love a rented house as their own.

8.4591.

I back off from women like from excessive expenses.

8.4627.

I've never met a divorced woman who would admit that she was guilty of the death of a relationship. Men are more self-critical in this way and sometimes admit their mistakes.

8.4628.

It's anyone else but herself that a woman blames for her problems. Weak men behave the same way.

8.4631.

The only way for a man to get rid of a woman is to replace her with another one or even with three at once.

8.4635.

Women want to be loved selflessly and the way they want to love their children who behave themselves and don't make them upset.

This desire is their vice... blind love for children turns them into vicious monsters. The same will happen to a woman who is loved blindly. If providence wanted a man to love a woman blindly, it would make it this way. Just the way it makes a man love her blindly at the stage of falling for her, however later it switches off this mode due to its serious danger for living.

8.4649.

When a woman belongs to her man, she becomes his extra source of energy and power as well as he does. In a system where she wants to keep her independence, the relationship of renting takes place. This way, a man is likely to lose energy. Here lies the eternal dispute about what is better, to buy a house or rent it. If you constantly move and change houses, renting is better. But as for a woman, it's not clear whether she needs an endless change of leaseholders.

8.4653.

The issue with smart women is that it's hard for them to admire stupid men, and they don't have accessible smart and single ones around them. This state of things spoils private life and quality of sex.

8.4659.

Generally, the concept of female freedom is profitable for men as it allows them not to get married and renting is less expensive than buying. Renting a woman is formally more profitable than buying her.

8.4669. Each of us belongs to someone.

Men belong to their ideas, passions and duties.
Women belong to their passions or men.
If a woman gets out of control by a man, she'll become a slave to her passions and pleasures. As a rule, it leads to being obsessed with yoga, fitness, some classes, work or family. Sometimes women can slaves to some ideas.

8.4731.

A woman doesn't have to think, she needs to feel.

8.4758.

Inflated self-respect turns a person into the own idol. Idols are vain and want others to serve them.

8.4764.

Talks about women's inflated self-respect are very useful for business. Family breakdowns are especially profitable for realtors, yoga-centers, restaurants, boutiques and many other organizations.

8.4772.

When a woman doesn't forgive a man for his mistakes, I call it betrayal.

8.4783.

God is a man while a woman is the creature of God. Though, perhaps everything was the other way round.
   Perhaps, it's not male God who created a woman, but a female Goddess created the world and then the man so that he would serve her...
   Female Goddess came down to Earth and became the first human being and progenitress of mankind.

8.4784.

It's more logical to suppose that mankind took origin from a woman rather than from a man. Women are able to reproduce without men, at least by conceiving through the Holy Spirit.

8.4787.

A man's natural function is to reproduce... In order to reproduce, it's necessary to have sex. That's why a woman who doesn't feel like having sex, makes a man awfully angry as he becomes unable to fulfil his mission because of her.

8.4795.

Prostitutes are the most honest kind of women.

8.4796.

Decent women are indecently expensive.

8.4812.

Taking into account the fact that a woman is God, then the more a man works for her the better his karma will be.

8.4813. When a woman loves you, God loves you as well.

When a man creates for women, it makes his karma much better... Thus, serving a woman is very useful as well, as when a woman loves you, God loves you as well.

8.4814.

It's more than likely that people took origin from a woman rather than from God. But perhaps, that woman was a female God.

8.4817.

It's typical of human beings to be mistaken. Since a woman is a direct descendent of God, she'd better forgive rather than make mistakes.

8.4822.

A woman who has work, yoga or fitness, doesn't need a husband.

8.4872.

A beautiful theory resembles a woman, she's so attractive that any other of her faults are insignificant.

8.5003.

If we take a look at the thought about beauty (perfection) as some paradoxical source of energy from the perspective of a relationship between a man and a woman, we'll see the following. A loved woman is always beautiful and perfect...Thus, it's very useful to serve her. The more a man loves or serves a loved or beautiful woman, the more energy she gives him. Beauty is in essence, God. It's necessary to worship beauty to make it stronger and more useful... beauty demands beautiful temples... Everyone should admire it. That's why a man should provide a loved woman with a beautiful house, car, clothes and entertainment... Should constantly provide her with traveling the whole world so that many people would see her and admire her. The more people admire her, the more energy a man will get. As beauty is very grateful to those who loves and serves it. Beauty is a great source of energy, happiness, good luck and pleasure.

An important moment- since happiness is a drug the dose of which should become heavier, you have to provide the constant growth and influence for the beauty you serve. Once you start it, you'll be unable to stop. If you betray your muse, you'll simply be damned.

8.5034.

Wasting money and time on a woman who doesn't love you is a useless and even dangerous loss of energy that will never be compensated and it's a sin.

8.5088.

Sex is a tool of enslavement by means of which a woman turns a man into her slave.

8.5090.

For a woman, sex is a great means of making a man work for her.

8.5128.

It's very dangerous to come together with women as breaking up with them later brings pain and expenses.

8.5178.

A beautiful woman is good, on the one hand (they give more energy and their power is stronger), but on the other hand, such woman is a source of many problems. Beauty is a great power, you will have to balance it with something, otherwise you'll be eaten...and you'll become its slave.

 Besides, beauty doesn't respect those who are weaker than it-self. So it will be difficult for you to hold it, a beautiful woman is a potential betrayer.

8.5179. A widow spider.

Are you scared of beautiful women? And rightly so, because if her beauty is stronger than you are, it will simply swallow you.

8.5191.

A prostitute is the one doing it without love, and money is what all women take.

8.5193. A graphite control rod of a nuclear reactor.

The task of a woman is to be a catalyzer, to inspire a man into actions, into conquering the world, into work and personal growth. Besides, she wants him not to burst out, not to make irrevocable mistakes and not to commit suicide out of depres-sion. The task of a muse is to keep a creator's working efficiency, helping him to create and cooling him off when he is so over-wrought that is ready to burst or go crazy.

8.5194. A muse is an engineer.

A muse is an engineer whose task is to let off steam, put wood into firebox, watch the road and control the engine so that it would go the right way and not try to explode or go get into the wrong place.

8.5233.

A frog is a woman too. And dreams about a prince too.

8.5267. One to three (four).

The variant «one man, one woman» is not really profitable for a man as it makes him dependent on one particular woman that may enslave him.

But this variant is not very profitable for a woman as well as once she loses it's her who will be the slave. But being in a threesome they would solve their problems better.

8.5281.

It's always a man who is to blame for a woman's power.

8.5282. There will be no exchange.

It's necessary to beware of strong women as they don't need men and thus, a man has nothing to offer to any of them.

8.5317.

A woman of the creator is a special type of woman, I call her Goddess. Can Goddess exist separately from God? - I doubt it.
   But the existence of God is also impossible without Goddess. What's more, GOD is the union of the essence of the creator and the essence of the goddess, the union of the male and female power.

8.5385.

Yoga and fitness are useful for women who got problems in personal life and don't have sex... They are substitutes for sex. As for many married women whose life lacks sex, it will be a nice substitute as well.

8.5638.

A woman is a drug, it's very difficult to start using a weaker drug after a strong one. After Mercedes going by bus would seem awfully boring.

8.5646. A woman is a majority of her own self.

There's always a lot of a woman. She's always so different. There are many women inside a woman. A woman is a matrix massif of many women...

8.5694. Women like extremes...

Women like either those who make them wonder or those who excite their pity... The function of women in this case is connected with the cultivation of extremes.

8.5702.

A loved woman is priceless, that's why a man who is in love is ready to pay any price even for the only hope to possess her.

8.571.1.

The main subjects for female aphorisms: complaining about difficulties in life and criticizing men, motivation into running away and changing lifestyle, demagogy about love, cultivation of peace, dreams about the sea and the desire to sleep well.

8.5729.

Before you make sure that a woman is yours, don't be jealous. Otherwise she will get offended and run away...

8.5740.

Dancing is some kind of drug for women and clubs are drug dens...

8.5741.

An independent woman is the one that it's better to have safe sex with... but getting married and starting a family with a woman of this kind would be a mistake.

8.5745. Rx only.

A woman resembles a medicinal agent, but just like any other remedies, she has plenty of negative side effects. It's necessary to take her exactly according to a dosing schedule. A woman can be recommended only for particular people and it's only a doctor who can prescribe her.

8.5748.

It's possible to deal with a woman but only until you become mad about her

8.5758.

A woman hears only what she wants to but not what they tell her... Besides, when she's angry she doesn't feel like getting anything good at all.

8.5759.

A woman is ready to hear and understand only the man she loves and only when she's not mad at him at the moment of speaking.

8.5763.

In a man's life, a woman performs the role of a graphite control rod of a nuclear reactor, she's a moderator and stabilizer.

8.5766. Women are a deceptive maneuver.

8.5770.

Women are necessary as they help to distract attention and resources from the main goal of men - seizure of the world.

8.5771.

If you decide to become a creator, take into account that you won't get on well with women as they demand love and you'll have to love your new world so that you won't have any extra love.

8.5788. Work saves from pain.

When your beloved woman leaves you, use it to your advantage. For example, you can become a workaholic and earn a powerful lot of money.

8.5817.

A muse is a curious angel, of course she will betray or leave you sooner or later and you will die of pain... but, first of all, your children will be with you and secondly, you'll be able to create even by using memories of her.

8.5819.

Well, I came to the conclusion that women should be let alone, let them do what they want. The main thing is not to fall for any of them.

8.5832.

It's easier to earn money than to charm a woman. But once you earn money, there won't be any need to charm women.

8.5836. Doomed to loneliness.

A man of art cannot be prescribed any women as art demands love and any woman dislikes it when there's someone else to love besides herself.

The same can be said about philosophers and those who are passionate about what they do- all of them are doomed to loneliness...

8.5841.

She's awfully angry with him as he hurts her. Her conscience is bothering her as she lies and cheats on him by not caring about his love and everything that he does for her...

8.5850.

Running after a woman when she runs away from you is not as funny as they describe in fiction...

8.5851. Or go to hell.

It's not noble to try to control a woman, it's better to let her do what she wants and may god help her.

8.5885.

Every man's heel of Achilles is some woman.

8.5899.

It's either you who should love your woman or someone else will do it so you'll die of jealousy.

8.5905.

By playing with love, a woman can easily break a man. A man should know his weaknesses and avoid hitting them. Men's weaknesses: jealousy, guilt, sex, a sense of Patriarchal and all that.

8.5917.

Emancipated women were created by sly men who really appreciate free love. An emancipated woman doesn't sell herself, and it's good as renting her is much cheaper...

8.5920.

Men are very displeased by hosting strangers on their territory, especially when it comes to their wives' relatives.

8.5943.

A woman feels bad without a man, and a man feels unbearably bad without a woman.

8.5949.

A woman should be loved, an unloved woman becomes very angry, even more angry than a man who also lacks love.

8.5982.

A woman is often aggressive with those who disturb her love.

8.5991.

A woman never gives in to the views she dislikes...

8.6009.

He held her dear because she costed him dear...

8.6077. A cat.

A woman stays with the one she feels good with. That's why if you need a woman, make her feel good... without any unnecessary questions... but remember that if someone offers her something better, she won't hesitate with her decision so work and try to make your offer the best one...

8.6078.

Do what you want but if you need a woman, make her happy and want for nothing, otherwise someone will attract her more and you'll die of pain.

8.6079.

Generally, a woman pays with her love for everything that a man does for her... Love is a drug, a man who loves is a drug addict.

8.6084.

She would like him to conquer her but according to the scenario she was supposed to resist angrily...

8.6143.

Even when a woman admits that she's wrong, it's nothing but cunning... deep in her heart she always remains impeccable...

8.6190.

Women like to run... Running is a great pleasure for them... Especially they prefer running from someone. But if you don't want to run after her, she will turn around and run after you...

8.6192.

By running away, she makes a man run after her... This way she rules him. But she got other ways of ruling as well. When a man doesn't feel like running, she turns around and attacks him in the attempt to hold control over her slave...

8.6217. There are two types of women - Muses and Witches.

A muse is the one who helps a dream come true. A witch is someone who prefers killing men's dreams. But both these two types coexist in every woman and it's a matter of her mood and general state of things which part of her is dominant at the moment.

8.6218.

Women have two tasks, the first is to kill male dreams and the second one is to make them come true really soon.

8.6245.

The essence of a foolish woman is not that men like her but that she likes men... And for a smart woman it's very difficult to find a man who wouldn't make her feel bored.

8.6295.

A man should never feel offended by a woman if he wants to save a relationship with her. Once he gets offended by a woman, she will be offended too and leave.

8.6376.

The more precious a woman is, the more she likes to task men's patience, looking for those who can pay more than others.

8.6522. In order to take, it's necessary to give first...

Female love and tenderness is a drug, it's necessary to make men addicted to it first and then charge an exorbitant price.

8.6570. A source of joy.

The main task of a woman is to be beautiful, anything else is optional.

8.6571. A working approach.

A man should treat a woman the way they teach women to treat men in women's magazines.

8.6654.

A beautiful woman is approximately the same as a rich man, there are few of them and they are powerful and impudent.

8.6658.

If a man is not a woman, he should not get offended by a woman.

8.6736.

A muse is the one who inspires a man into miracles.

8.6746.

One shouldn't blame women for anything, but you can blame yourself for being stupid enough to deal with them.

8.6797.

If a woman loves you, she's useful. If she doesn't, run away to survive.

8.6838.

It's difficult for a brainy woman to love a brainless man. But as is known, a man is mad about the woman he loves. That's why female brains damage personal life.

8.6908.

It's better to treat women with suspicion. The more suspicious a woman is, the better.

8.6999.

A woman resembles the Moon, if you want her to get into your orbit you should be much bigger than her. The strategy is simple: you carefully get closer to her, freeze and wait what will happen. But be careful not to get too close, the collision of two planets may destroy both of them.

8.7001.

It's wrong to chase a woman by obsessive stalking. The effect is the opposite. For every action there is a reaction. You'd better give a woman some space for moving towards yourself, otherwise she will run away in the opposite direction.

8.7026.

Women like to kill love and then sue the dead one for alimony.

8.7032.

A woman is jumpy, a man should twitch less.

8.7039.

Beautiful women demand great patience from men.

8.7040.

Beautiful women are very unstable, she will be taken before you know it.

8.7088. Press until it goes click.

A man can't count on anything until something inside a woman clicks.

8.7129.

There's nothing more useful for a woman than a man who is guilty towards her.

8.7246.

People really like the emptiness of thoughts as it's possible to fill it with anything.

8.7247.

Vague words can be interpreted in an arbitrary fashion, which on the one hand makes them lose any meaning, but on the other hand fills them with any desired meaning.

8.7272.

It's necessary to get a woman talking, it's a big pleasure for a woman. Talking is pleasurable for a person.

8.7345.

Without a real woman there's no real man. A woman is the person who defines the essence of a man right from his birth till his death.

8.7368.

Beautiful women have difficulties in personal life. Beauty is power and a woman needs a man who is stronger than herself so that to admire him. However, it's a big problem to drive such a man crazy as the power of a man is money and wits which make a man quite cynical and hypocritical, and thus, barely suitable for love.

8.7371.

A woman should either drive a man crazy or leave him as someone genetically incompatible with her.

8.7455.

Women like to raise argument but dislike being argued with.

8.7475.

A man needs a dream and a woman needs a man with a dream.

8.7477. A toad.

Since there are no other particular variants, girls like to play the roles of princesses (fairies) or little witches.

8.7494.

I've noticed that many people and especially women are unable to distinguish dreams from reality. Then what is the difference between them?

8.7501. Femme fatale.

She's very deep, lovers sink in her and the drowned float to the surface.

8.7511.

A woman doesn't even care whether a man that she loves is lousy, her own feelings and pleasure that she gets from him are more important to her and she doesn't want to lose it all.

8.7513.

Women hate chauvinists but all men are chauvinistic, that's why successful men are very hypocritical and have many different masks to choose from for every particular person they ever deal with.

8.7514. Female method.

If a man deliberately maintains distance from a woman he dates, it means he tries to manipulate her and evoke her passion to get control over her.

8.7518. A ghoul.

It's terribly disadvantageous for a woman to date a man who doesn't love her... And thus, the one who is not mad about her... As it's only a loving man who cares and respects his woman, but a pretender is hypocritical and hates his victim and only uses her.

8.7521.

Women are very simple... no need to reinvent wheels. Be good but keep distance and they will break chains... only to get you. Light hunger evokes strong passion in them.

8.7522.

The peculiarity of women is that even once they realize the manipulation done over them, they still stay under its influence as women are slaves to their desires... And if some NLP manipulation evokes a desire in a woman, it no longer matters whether she sees it or not. That's why women are affected even by such primal manipulations like mirroring and direct nonsense like throwing dust in someone's eyes.

8.7523. They deserve each other.

It's important to realize that a woman can be a slave to sex under the condition that she does it with the man she loves. Sex with the one she loves switches off a woman's brain. That's why before having sex with a woman it's useful for a man to make her fall for him and to do that it's enough to be caring and uncritical and keep some distance to make her slightly hungry.

However, a man in love is brainless too.

8.7524.

Sex is a tool of a woman to control a man she loves, no need to waste such a precious resource on men who are not in love with her.

8.7548.

If she wants she will believe any nonsense.
If she doesn't want to, even pure truth won't help.

8.7554.

Men and women deserve each other, I wouldn't idealize any-one, because as is known, of every living thing of all flesh there should be two of every sort. And you should remember that if you don't find the living thing of your sort, you will die out.

8.7558.

If a woman doesn't feel like doing something, don't make her do it, otherwise everything will be unpredictably bad.

8.7562.

Any decent man (aka genius, sunlight, hero or simply alfa male) is a psycho doomed to self-destruction. But a woman-muse who is able to save him and turn him into sunlight- nuclear reactor as she will perform the role of graphite rods in the nuclear reactor and will help to escape an explosion and make the system work usefully.

8.7563.

On the one hand, women dislike psychos, but on the other hand, they simply can't use them properly... In essence, a psycho is the most useful type of man... a man "nuclear reactor", a man "sun-light" and a source of energy. The essence of a woman's art is about ruling a man to escape an explosion and self-destruction of the energetic pattern. It can be supposed that in the system where a man is a nuclear reactor, a woman is fuel- uranium and at the same time a ruling graphite rod.

8.7712.

A man will never hit a natural woman, while he should avoid unnatural ones.

8.7742.

Don't touch a woman during her PMS, simply don't touch her...

otherwise she will bite you...

8.7785.

A woman is very dangerous, but even the fact that a man is aware of the danger she may cause, doesn't stop him from being mad about her once she gets closer with him. In essence, the only means of struggling is to keep an artificial distance and not let a woman intrude on his feelings so that to control them.

8.7798.

If a man sees a woman as an enemy, he will soon get into evolutionary dead end... and will die out like a mammoth. A woman is not an enemy but rather an aim.

8.7800. A monk.

An ocean of energy will be available for a man if he manages to stay away from women.

8.7811.

The problem is not that women became worse but that men are no longer strong and smart enough to inspire women into love.

8.7819.

The fact that a woman doesn't want to belong to a man is not her problem, but rather a problem of a man who is too weak or stupid to own her.

8.7856.

The best method of controlling overpopulation is pathos. The more females are full of pathos, the less they want to reproduce.

8.7861.

The stronger, smarter and more independent a woman is, the more difficult it is for her to find a man who would inspire her into reproduction.

On the other hand, such state of things speeds up evolution and gives the best men a huge priority for reproduction, while the worst ones die out. Now, when a woman is independent and able to feed her offspring on her own, the best males are able to have tens of children born by different women.

8.8034.

If a woman is beautiful or rich, she will definitely be courted by decent men and will be able to choose the best one. But if a woman is not of high quality, then she'd better be active herself so that to try to get some more or less decent candidate for reproduction. Otherwise, she will have to deal with low-quality genetic material and it will influence her future family life and children and in a negative way.

8.8035. A homeless fledgling sparrow.

He fell for her because she gave him one while others refused. But then another one gave him one and he suddenly fell for her and forgot about the first one.

8.8036. A hungry chaffinch.

Nobody ever loved him, but this woman gave him one. Of course, soon he fell for her.

8.8039. Lookers-on see more than players.

A usual female delusion "I'm not like this, I'm another type" is also typical of men. It's better to eradicate this in yourself and don't resist attempts to become a cultured person.

8.8052. Love overcomes any problems.

A desire resembles a woman, so if you want it you'll have to love it, serve it, conquer it and do your best to deserve it... You need it to choose you and love you... And here much depends on the desire itself, on the competition level and on yourself.

8.8086. A scene taken from a movie.

Women like to be kissed on the neck and shoulders, because firstly, it's romantic and beautiful and secondly, it happens only from time to time.

8.8118. Peace is a pleasure resulting from the absence of fear and worries.

As for women, stability is their greatest pleasure and source of peace. Daily repetitiveness of rituals, particular words, gestures, kisses, hugs- all of it is important, any change or infrequency of these ritual actions may become a source of worry that disturbs the mind.

8.8120. A sacred morning kiss.

Women are very sensitive to respond to changes for the worse. They tend to stabilize the system and not let it go down for the worse.

8.8126. The best strategy of survival.

Women choose the best (in their opinion) patterns and follow them as long as they work, without looking for anything better when all is good enough.

8.8139.

A woman loves a man because she feels good near him and bad when he's not around.

8.8145.

Male and female brains differ in interests. They are interested in totally different things, and we remember: the brain considers anything uninteresting as a stupid thing.

8.8158.

A woman appreciates a man for the feelings she gets when he is near.

8.8252. An unstable radioactive isotope.

A woman who loves a man's money and not himself, should be ignored. It's not a matter of morality or expenses, but rather a matter of this woman's instability. Because as soon as she finds a bigger source of energy (even a good job), soon she will become a betrayer.

8.8349.

A woman can have various goals and strategies in life, but the most classical one is to find a man who is decent enough for reproduction. She needs a potentially best man, a man with a dream, a unique man who will be able to find his place (a natural niche) in life, and use it to get the access to energy. While a woman, by performing the role of the muse, should encourage his man into moving towards his dream and the more unique and epic this dream is, the better.

8.8389.

Beautiful women can be of two types: they are either loved or really beautiful.

8.8456.

Why do all cartoon princesses have really big eyes? Are they cows or insects?

8.8513.

Women are very useful because they create the greatest value of this world called men.

8.8517.

Children are a source of pure energy for their parents. It's nature and children that can give energy to a woman, and later a woman can share this energy with her man or use it for work.

8.8520. I can't help loving women...

An overwhelming feeling
excitement of the heart
And I want to embrace it...
And any doubts die out...

8.8544.

A woman largely depends on her hairstyle. It can be said that a woman's mode of thinking largely depends on her looks.

8.8600. A woman is a useful resource.

For a man everything is easier at home, while women are more mobile and useful everywhere and for everyone.

8.8692. Silly hope.

It seems to me that the only thing that can save mankind from dying out is women. They are the only creatures who can theoretically stop men from getting lost in virtual game worlds. However, if virtual worlds offer paradise and all-inclusive package, then obviously this hope is silly.

8.8707. About the use of feminism, female freedom and independence.

Feminism is profitable for men. Feminism is the practice of renting a woman and not owning her. In former times, it took being the owner of a woman to have sex with her, now it's unnecessary. Now when a woman is more free and independent, she becomes easier. Now men can easily satisfy their eternal need to have sex with different women, now there are enough women for all men and it's not necessary to marry or generally love becomes a cheaper thing. In other cases, men would have to live without women's love and it would make men really angry and unruly which would be bad for society.

8.8708. The practice of polygamy.

Polygamy is not profitable for most men and the government. In case of mass practice of polygamy there won't be enough women for men and it will lead to great social indignation. A woman is a tool for ruling and controlling a man, if there are not enough women so that some men are left without women, these men will soon become totally unruly and socially dangerous.

8.8728.

We associate women with love and tenderness. But people are full of contradictions and extremes, that's why it's love that makes women very cruel. One extreme leads to another one, but an opposite one.

8.8734.

Women are biologically better at getting incoming (external) information than men.

8.8777.

Women are a very strong kind of demons who should not be given freedom. However, it's not clear whether anyone should be given freedom as it may turn anyone into a demon. Freedom breeds demons.

8.8795.

It's only a woman who can save a family, it's useless to count on a man in this case.

8.8807.

I wouldn't recommend you to marry a very beautiful woman, wouldn't recommend to marry a very young girl... I wouldn't recommend you to marry at all but... I myself did everything another way.

8.8852.

Ideas resemble women. They are ready to give themselves to those who will serve them, love them or give energy (money) for their realization. But it's important to know your price and at least remain morally stable in public.

8.8859. The strategy of a muse.

This world is ruled by heroes, bu it's muses who create heroes. It's up to a woman to create a hero out of the man she loves. Heroes work miracles and perform feats, they can rule time and money. In other words, if a woman needs miracles and money, she'd better find her personal man and make him a hero.

8.913.1.

Two main female problems are men and chronic lack of sleep.

8.913.2. The main fetish.

I've got the feeling that women got nothing else to dream about but the sea.

8.913.3. A she-eggplant.

The main female dream is to become a vegetable, namely a she-eggplant. The sea, sand, all inclusive, and you lie in the sun and do nothing while slowly turning into a she-eggplant.

9.1041.

Sales and advertising are the process of seduction, the product is a beautiful woman, driving a man crazy.

9.1650.

A dream is like a beautiful woman, it should be won over.

9.1677.

A woman is an energy amplifier, she multiplies everything, the good and the bad alike.

9.2260.

After marrying off your daughter, lock the doors. Women are fearful, once she has somewhere to retreat, she will run back for sure. However, if she has nowhere to retreat, she will find the strength to build a house of her own.

9.2270.

Women strongly dislike being taught. Women's knowledge come from observation of reality, therefore they like watching and feeling phenomena more than listening to somebody's lecturing and teaching them.

9.2326. Technology of hassling.

Repeating the same request constantly, you can make a person do whatever you want.

9.2573.

It's true that women are closer to money than men. By feeling reverence for women, especially for his wife, a man can really become rich. God loves those who love women.

9.2575.

A happy wife in the house draws money to the house.

9.3439.

Women are not loved by those who they don't love. Those, who are loved by women, cannot resist these wonderful creatures.

9.3457.

There are less women than men in business not because of male chauvinism, but because women don't like risking.

9.3469. Doomed whatever the case

Let us be honest, a man does not need a woman, for she is dangerous and harmful, the only problem is that without a woman, he feels even worse.

9.3491.

Feminism was thought up by men who disapproved of their women's sponging on them and not working.

9.3605.

Girls like being taught, while men like teaching. It is impossible to know if this eagerness to knowledge is sincere in women or they simply like the attention, however for men a chance to show their intelligence is a great joy.

9.3608. Support of power.

Women, like electors, conserve the social relations and tend to support the acting authority. Women are conservative and so-cial-minded, easily prone to the influence of mass media, they prefer stability and strong leaders.

9.3771.

Women like romance and courtship just as in books and films therefore avoid inventing wheels, you'd better study the pri-mary sources.

9.3772.

Girls prefer gallant men, who do not forget to praise their new hairstyle, their nails or their dress.

9.3781.

Never let a girl be bored in your company, you'd better be quick and lively, than slow and dull.

9.3788.

A delicious smell works up your appetite, and the same goes for beauty.

9.3985.

Women are more prone to fears than men. One of the basic purposes of the female organism is reproduction. A healthy and strong body is required for this. A woman's health and integrity can be harmed by anything, that is why women tend to be afraid of everything. In principle, it is quite normal, when within reasonable limits. However, problems arise when mind ends and all kinds of phobias, paranoias and panic attacks arise.

The majority of women like safety and stability, recesses and comfort, they hate to attract the crowd's attention, dislike threats to their health and life, dislike being scolded and criticized, dislike changes. Threats to their inward peace cause neuroses and hormonal problems to them.

On the other hand, everything may be vice versa. The soul yearns for everything to be the other way round, then the person may fall into the opposite extreme (we remember that there always are three extremes and one may choose any of them). It is curious that in the system with everything vice versa, health problems and neuroses will be caused by stagnation and safety, while dangers, on the contrary, will give rise to vivacity and gaiety.

9.4603.

Not only men fight for women, but women fight for men, too. Everybody aims at perfection. If a person is the perfection, both men and women will fight for the right to be near him.

9.4694. Women and dreams.

You will lose everything that you will lose interest in. No interest, no love, no love – no relationship.

9.4986.

A woman is either a super guide and a Muse or resistance, i.e. a

Witch. By resisting a man, she makes him stronger. Furious that he is interfered with, the man finds within himself enormous strength to do everything the other way round. Men like to overcome difficulties and they feel inspired when they have an enemy. They seek freedom by acting the other way around.

9.7594. Negative and positive woman.

Many women are aware of their social suggestibility. They know that they want to follow the example of other women. And, as a means of combating this phenomenon, they begin to act from the opposite, turning their reaction and doing the opposite. Now, if someone likes something, they don't like it. Such women prefer something very specific and strange. They like to feel special.

In fact, the positive and negative way of thinking is fundamentally no different from each other and are special cases of collective social reason.

10.5791.

Women make men tender and cowardly. Being attached to female caress, the man becomes weak.

10.6475.

In social animals, especially in females, there is a fear of loneliness in the soul, which determines all their social activity.

10.6965.

The easiest way to fall in love with a girl is to start pulling her pigtails... In girls, the main thing is to attract her attention. A girl will feel like a hero if she tames or defeats a boy who offends her. Having won the boy with love, the girl will automatically fall in love with him.

10.6966.

Let them conquer you with love, and they will fall in love with you.

10.7003. Long dress

"Everything about you is fine," king Solomon once remarked to the Queen of Sheba, "but your legs are hairy... not my type."

10.7092. Eggs and mice.

They say women are divided into chickens and cats. I know you like cats, but smart people choose chickens.

10.7202.

Women are gentle and fear the cold, which makes them cowardly and dependent.

10.7203.

A woman with her aggression and boorish attitude to people expresses her loneliness. She wants to attract the attention of a strong man who could overcome her loneliness and save her from suffering.

10.7239. Dad, be human!!!

A woman always expects from a man what her father could not give her... it is Useful to choose a wife that the father does not love very much, otherwise you will break down.

10.7245.

Femininity is a willingness to cooperate.

10.7366. Hugs.

The power of a woman is that she can use both her own and a man's weapon if she wants to. It is very difficult for a man to use a woman's weapon.

10.7411. Girls love with their ears.

In Russian, the word "lover" has a beautiful synonym-boyfriend.

A suitor is someone who talks a lot.

10.7414. Don't push it.

Nadezhda is a modest girl, she requires delicacy, but consistency of effort.

10.7474. A woman full of doubts.

The problem with many women is that, first of all, they do not love themselves, but they want to be loved. And second, they do not know what love is, so they constantly doubt whether they are loved or not.

10.7606.

The girl's relationship with her father is very curious. Having learned to manage her father, to add to his love, ... the girl fulfills the skills that she will later apply to her husband.

10.7710.

Neither fish nor meat are mushrooms. There are some women we call the pale toadstool. Toadstools are deadly poisonous to men and unsuitable for living together.

10.7844.

Women are easy, listen to them, do what they want, and you will be happy. Women's desires are simple and pleasant. You yourself will like to be a performer of women's desires.

10.7849. In search of attention.

If a man goes into his problems and forgets about his woman, the woman intuitively does everything possible to become his problem.

10.7850. The only problem.

When a man suffers from an overflow of problems, a woman intuitively does everything possible to make him forget about all her problems.

10.7853.

Women know the value of their words and therefore do not believe men's words, but wait for action. Words are hope, faith is action.

10.7854.

Hug, say that everything will be fine, massage the feet of the paws, rustle in the hair, bring delicious... words should be supported by actions. Actions are courage, women in men love courage.

10.7860.

Are you sure you want to kill her? Are you sure you're afraid of her? A woman tries to convey to you that she wants love and affection, but you listen to your fears instead. Don't be afraid of women, women are afraid of everything ...they doubt everything, etc. she needs a man to kill her fears and doubts, say: "Everything will be fine" ... Hug and all that...

10.7876.

A woman needs a man she can admire, she needs a beast. If a woman begins to doubt that her man is a beast, she will provoke and try to Wake the beast in him. A Woman in a man needs a fierce fire, because love and fire are one and the same thing.

10.7881.

When you're afraid, you lie, women don't like men who are liars.

10.7883. Love is courage.

If a man loves, the fear inside him disappears, and the woman, seeing his love, automatically falls in love with him. Women know that love is when there is no fear.

10.7886.

Do not be afraid of a woman, as long as you are afraid of her, she will not be able to love you.

10.7887.

Mirror it... She raises her voice and you raise your voice. She's joking and you're joking... But do it with gambling joy and feel it... Her pain, not his... Forget yourself, forget it. It hurts her, and it hurts you, because it hurts her... She's furious and you're furious... You are one.

10.7909.

When a man goes headlong into his problems, a woman goes mad with pain from loneliness and puts him before a choice: problems or her. A man in love should say that all problems are nonsense, and turn his attention to the woman.

10.7911.

You should take care of a woman not out of fear and with fear, but with joy. Treat your love with passion. Excitement is the cure for fear.

10.7924.

A woman loves her hero. And it is unbearably painful for her when a man ceases to match this image. You can not lie, the hero is honest, kind, caring, open and courageous. Lying breeds fear, cowardice, closeness, aggression, contempt for people, pride, etc.

10.7930.

Women expect attention from men, not self-pity. When a man loves only his problems and fears, women do not like this.

10.7936.

If a woman is angry, it means that she is tired of being a man, and wants her man to become a man himself.

10.7937.

It's very easy with women, you hold her hand and tell her how much you love her, how everything will be fine.

10.7938.

Empathy is when you feel the feelings of another person, not your own fear or joy. Women feel other people's feelings, and men usually focus on their own. If there is no fear inside the man, the woman loves him, if there is fear, it is transmitted to the woman, mixed with her fear and generates an explosion.

10.7939.

Fear is inside the woman. A woman's empathy is related to the fact that she runs from her fear to find a place where there is no fear, but there is confidence. Next to a confident man, a woman feels like behind a stone wall, living in his soul. If a man has fear, the woman is caught between two fires-her own and his fear. The sense of security, confidence, self-esteem falls, and the woman falls into horror. A woman can't stand men's fear.

10.7940.

When a man hides his fear in front of a woman, he does not explain what he is afraid of... the woman, feeling his fear, but not understanding his nature, becomes terrified and begins to attack.

10.7945.

A woman, finding a confident man, empathically perceiving his confidence, gets rid of her fears and falls into joy and euphoria. But once a woman feels a man's fear, an ocean of darkness immediately descends on her and the magic ends.

10.7952.

Girl templates. It is, among other things, feels solubleness and loss of autonomy. Violation of the template "for 3 months of marriage": according to its template, at least a year and a half should pass. Violation of the template torments and seriously fuels thoughts about the error of the decision.

10.7960.

It is desirable for a man to match the dreams of his woman in order to deserve her admiration. Female admiration is very invigorating and motivating.

10.7967.

Multicolored women look like flowers. It seems like spring has come.

10.7989.

A woman gets more pleasure from sex than a man, not because she has some special receptors in the vagina, but because she empathically multiplies her pleasure and the partner. By focusing on her own and someone else's pleasure, she is completely cleared of fears and unnecessary thoughts, which further increases the joy.

10.8004. Feelings and desires.

An active male position is when a man offers a woman options for what she wants. The fact is that a woman does not know what she wants, which is why she needs a man. A man who constantly asks a woman what she wants causes irritation in a woman. It's better to ask how she feels about the options offered to her.

10.8006.

Empathy is a woman's feeling, because it makes a person run away from himself, makes him dependent on a stronger one. It is empathy that makes women dependent on men. A strong and courageous man is selfish and withdrawn.

10.8008. Symbiotic system.

In order for an empathic woman not to go crazy with fear and suspiciousness, she needs a courageous, self-centered, strong man who does not know fear. A self-confident man will save a woman from fear and uncertainty, and a woman will inspire him and convey empathic information about the world around him.

10.8011.

A manly man will not even raise an eyebrow when he sees a beautiful woman, but he will be kind and affectionate, for there is no fear in him. Such restraint, like a magnet, will attract a woman to him.

10.8012. Participation in creation.

A woman is a cold moon inside herself, which warms a man from the inside, generates volcanic activity in him and a craving for life and creation. The moon is awfully fond of looking at the earth and contemplating the creation of life. Lunar empathy is participation in life.

10.8013.

A woman feels fear empathically and is sensitive to fear. And a man is insensitive and courageous, this protects him from fear. In order for a woman not to go mad with fear, she needs an insensitive, self-confident man, and a man needs to trust his woman to get information about threats and trends in the outside world. At the same time, a man should clearly understand that in General this information is exaggerated by an order of magnitude and it is not necessary to indulge all the fears and desires of his woman.

10.8017.

A man is very useful for a woman, because he helps her make

decisions and do not doubt anything. A man's self-confidence warms a woman's mind with its stability.

10.8020.

A woman, feeling the admiring attention of a man, is happy. Admiration is joy, joy for a woman like a drug.

10.8021.

Young and beautiful women are especially aggressive and daring, because they want to attract a manly man who has no fear and scare away cowards.

10.8145.

A man needs to think because he doesn't feel anything. And a woman does not need to think, she has an intuition that thinking only hinders, generating unnecessary fears.

10.8198.

If a woman is given the opportunity to take an active position, for example, by giving the right and opportunity to offer options, she will rejoice, finding freedom from fear.

10.8224.

Doubt is a woman's property. The firmness of the decision is a man's property. Doubt breeds fear.

10.8227.

Women are full of doubts and love men who know how to overcome their doubts.

10.8295.

You need to listen to your wife's criticism, her wife will not say nonsense. A wife wants to be proud of her husband and is extremely traumatized when her husband spoils from all sorts of different vices and sins.

10.8390.

A woman wants and doesn't want at the same time. You can help one of the parties, and it will easily win.

10.8391.

In the conquest of a woman, you should combine and alternate strategies of starvation, retreat, and new violent attacks. Given the duality of a woman's consciousness, you should strive to support her second Self, which is allied to you.

10.8392.

A distraction strategy works best in winning over a woman. Working together for your or her benefit is like love that connects.

10.8404.

The reason for women's sorrows is women's joy. The joys of women are so strong and intoxicatingly beautiful that in their absence the rest of the world becomes disastrously sad.

10.8447.

Women who have given birth, guess that all sorts of life problems, fear and pain are all insignificant little things of life.

10.8458.

After parting, the woman cries for three days, and then the click and as a hand removed. This happened habituation and the emergence of immunity. "Well, that's all," the woman rejoices, " I'm free." The main thing in this case is not to restrain your heartaches, the more pain, the sooner you get used to it.

10.8596. A slap in the face to public taste...

I have noticed that it is useful for a woman to start a conversation with a slap in the face in order to attract a strong man... In the second stage, it will be useful to cry or gently bandage the injured person.

10.8628. Support the game

If a woman insists on provoking a scandal, do not deny her this pleasure.

10.8633.

Most managers and women have a well-developed empathy and are sensitive to fear, inattention, lies, lack of order and beauty...

10.8763.

Rage kills fear... and that's good. But a man's rage awakens love in a woman... this is also good.

10.8858. The hero is joyful.

When a girl is shy, it makes the boys feel like a hero. Boys like to feel like heroes in shy girls. Acquaintances and friends also love these girls, because they feel especially bold against their background.

10.8862. A witch in a woman must be loved.

Every woman has a witch, if a woman doesn't have a witch, it's not a woman at all ... If you don't see a woman as a witch, you'll have to find a witch in her... otherwise you'll make a woman lie to herself. Lying creates fear, and instead of loving you, a woman will fear you and even hate you.

10.9086.

A woman from lack of attention spoils her health and mood. A man from lack of attention becomes angry or cowardly.

10.9288.

A man dreams of a woman who would support him in all his feelings, even in mistakes, depressions, failures and despair. A woman, in turn, dreams of a man who does not need to be supported, because the man is healthy and heavy, and the woman is weak and fragile.

10.9290.

A mother and daughter who live together often fight, because the more unhappy a woman is, the faster a hero will be found who will want to save her from Baba Yaga. Women adore heroes who save them from all universal evil.

10.9291.

For a woman to find a man, first she needs to find a problem. When a woman has a problem, finding a hero to save princesses from dragons is a no-brainer.

10.9336. Sunshine.

Against the background of strong chronic fear, many people, especially women, run away to pathological optimism and fantasy worlds that are extremely far from reality. In their fantasies, these individuals think of themselves as heroes and rulers of reality.

10.9337. Love is enlightenment.

The sleeping beauty metaphor can be seen as a woman living in a world of her own illusions until she falls in love. Love brings a woman back to reality. Love is the awakening from a dream into the real world. A woman escapes from fear into the world of her illusions, and only love, saving her from fear, allows her to return back to reality.

10.9346.

The sleeping beauty metaphor is an image of a woman living far from reality, in a world of her own fantasies and illusions. Only love can bring a woman back to reality, forcing her to live here and now.

10.9453.

Neither fish nor meat is a mermaid woman who lives in the depths of her illusions. There is no love in this woman, and therefore she is extremely far from reality. Why is there no love in it? Fear killed her love... monsters and dragons have deprived her of her freedom and imprisoned her in the tower of her illusions, but there is no Prince who would come and save his Princess from fear.

10.9461.

The mermaid is a metaphorical image of a woman who lives forever in the half-sleep of her illusions. Returning to reality causes a woman pain that only love can justify. In the absence of love, a woman is either "neither fish nor meat" or an evil fury going mad with pain and anger.

10.9462.

Jean and the mermaid are very similar metaphorical images that live in the dream of their illusions. Reality causes them pain that only love can save them from. If Gina or the mermaid Wake up and not give them love, they will go wild with fear and pain.

10.9530.

A proud, strong woman, meeting a man who has fear, may become fixated that her mission in life is to help him get rid of fear.

10.9533.

A woman needs a man she can manage, in the sense that he can grow under her sensitive guidance. A woman is a gardener who likes something to grow.

10.9541.

A woman often confuses an unsatisfied desire for power with

love. Sensing her victim, the woman reaches out to her, unable to control herself. A woman feels her victims through fear and weakness. It's like a Panther scenting a wounded deer. He's not a lodger – he's a Panther, and he can't leave him alone.

10.9566.

Women love monsters... The reason is banal, all men are monsters, so there is no special choice. Moreover, if a man hides his monster too much, he will be suspected of hypocrisy and lies. Lying is what kills love.

10.9727.

A woman likes an aggressive man. He swears, the woman cries, he is tormented by remorse, he seeks peace... Women take over. The hero who defeated the monster is joyful.

8.1306.2.

It's difficult for a strong woman to find a man who would be stronger than her fears.

8.1715.4.

Just like women, money likes beautiful things and smart strong men.

8.1901.5. Female cheating is many times worse than male.

The problem of more responsibility and unacceptability of female cheating is that a woman can easily get pregnant from another man but it's her husband who will have to feed and bring up this cuckoo fledgling as well as give him family budget later. Plus, as long as a wife is pregnant with this cuckoo fledgling, she can't get pregnant from her husband. Such perspective can make any sensible man mad and furious. Besides, there are many other reasons provided against female cheating and there's nothing unfair or inequal about it.

8.1902.1.

An interesting thought about cheating.
Of course, female cheating is bad and full of big problems for women themselves. But let's see why it happens. And why nature gave women such an opportunity.
A woman can cheat not for nothing but for some ego boost. It's not just anyone she may choose but only the best of the available "stud muffins". Of course, a "wild stud" will never marry her and will never become a domestic draught horse but she likes his fresh blood and good genes. A woman can easily fall in love with such a stud and may get pregnant from him. Nature craves for genetic diversity and the culmination of best people. And the fact that a woman will later give birth to a cuckoo fledgling and her husband will have to feed them all, coincides with the idea of working bees and ants. It's genetically best beings who provide future generations while others are meant to work and feed them. Such state of things coincides with the evolution ideas about maximal distribution of the most perfect or diverse genetic code.
As for the diverse genetic issues, it can be noticed that the more genetic differences there are between a man and a woman, the better it is. In ancient times it looked the following way. One day some traveler came from afar and stayed on the occupied territory without any means of survival. But his genetics seemed useful for the local individuals. Some female liked this traveler and got ready to get pregnant from him so that the old male in the local community would feed the newborn and let it raise on his territory. Thus, he would become the owner of resources who would feed "novelty" and "fresh blood". Or "perfection", as women like to deal with the best of available males like bosses or some "people person" or unofficial leaders.
Thus, seen from morality and family perspective, female cheating is a bad thing but considered from evolutionary ad genetic perspective it's a good thing.

8.1902.2.

Indeed, women cheat with the best "studs" to boost their spirits and ego. And it's clear that a woman will never leave her domestic bull and that a "stud" will never marry her but she likes the idea to get pregnant from the best male even if it's her domestic donkey who will have to feed the cuckoo fledgling and perform household chores... Even if he's not a stud who evokes the desire to get pregnant from him (and sex with him is boring), but at least it's possible to yoke him and make him work, which is impossible with studs.

8.2150.3.

Husbands should not criticize their wives as wives are the reflections of their husbands. Show me your wife and I'll tell who you are.

10.10116.

In order for a woman to fall in love with a man, he needs an Achilles heel of weakness in order to make a woman feel power over him. A woman should be lured by the opportunity to dominate.

10.10136.

A woman inspires a man with her faith. When the whole world is against you and defeats rain down on your head... a woman's love will become a sun in the ocean of darkness, an endless source of power and energy.

10.10153. Iron motivator.

A woman can motivate a man to overcome any Vice, problem, fear, laziness and uncertainty with her faith and love, anger and tears.

10.10160. You to me, I to you.

It is quite easy for a woman to stop loving, for this she builds a wall of iron arguments that her former man is not suitable for her and is harmful. To do this, she learns and parses her former love into puzzles and, having deprived her of the riddle, she defends herself from it with his own weapon. The essence of this proof: to prove that love is not there and never was, which means that there was a lie and a mistake.

10.10202. Unity of Yin and Yang.

Women are dominated by the need to complete the Gestalt, that is, to form patterns and complete forms. In men, the desire for knowledge and expansion dominates. By connecting, a woman and a man achieve harmony... a man captures new territories, and a woman motivates the construction of new walls and borders. Women are formulaic and limited in thinking. Men, on the contrary, do not recognize patterns and restrictions.

10.10278.

The desire to give advice and teach others is a desire to increase one's own importance and amuse one's inferiority complex. In fact, this is a sign of weakness. This is especially harmful when dealing with women, women do not like weak men. Women have enough of their own weaknesses.

10.10285.

A man looks like a deceptive peacock through a woman's eyes. These poor flying birds are always trying to look better than they really are.

10.10353.

Sleeping beauty will not Wake up, she sleeps, being in the deep belief that the Prince will appear and awaken her with a magic kiss.

10.10564.

Woman is the soft that surrounds the hard, dominating it. A man is a solid that fills the soft.

10.10683. Unisex.

For corporations, a woman is more profitable than a man. Since the world is ruled by corporations, which are the main source of energy for people, this generates evolutionary processes aimed at increasing femininity in males.

10.10873.

Women are passive in love, in the sense that they are very important perspective in the relationship. That is, women do not love a man so much as they like growth as a symbol of life and belonging to it.

10.11466.

A woman perceives jealousy in her address, on the one hand, as aggression and an attempt to deprive her of her freedom, and on the other hand, as a manifestation of love and a positive act. The second effect is intuitive.

10.11708.

A woman who chooses a man out of a subconscious desire to dominate him will be very disappointed with the relationship, because power is ephemeral and involves a struggle.

10.12016.

It is very important for a woman to feel small but powerful. A woman knows that she is not a head, but she wants to dominate – like a neck. A man needs to give a woman the illusion of power, otherwise she will go mad with fear and be offended. The consequences can be very sad from chronic pain to suspiciousness and divorce.

10.12189.

When a woman becomes pregnant, her overall level of fear

decreases against the background of fears associated with the child.

10.12330.

A man calls a woman to play, she can't refuse. Women love games, they love being played with. Feel like Alice rushing down the rabbit hole, this is a favorite women's game.

10.12363.

It is unbearably boring for a woman to love a man without a dream. Feeling the devotion of the man of her dreams, the woman understands – whether there is love in the man and whether his dream is real. If a woman likes a man's dream, then such a man can be loved.

10.12834.

The taming of the shrew is that the one she falls in love with must ignore her.

10.12913.

A woman (mother), observing her man (child), keenly feels good and evil. Evil is idleness, passivity, vices and dependencies, megalomania, negativism, aggressiveness and contempt for the world around us.

10.12954. Fair balance.

Only a proud man can love a proud woman. On the contrary, respectively, too. These two are created to drink blood and ruin each other's lives. Proud people can only love each other, they simply despise all other people. On the other hand, minus by minus gives a plus. Over time, when the fire burns out, these two have a chance to find humility.

10.13020.

A woman can save a boy from pride and voluptuousness by

limiting his pleasure and access to sex. In the absence of a woman, a man will deteriorate from an overabundance of Masturbation.

10.13196.

A woman provokes a man to physical violence by psychological violence.

10.13268.

A proud woman wants to love only the one over whom she feels her power.

10.13402.

Men, of course, are proud demons, creatures of the very depths of hell, but don't think that women are much better. Woman is the moon, the cause of the volcanic activity of the planet Earth. The Moon is responsible for the atmosphere and climate on our planet.

10.13825.

More than anything, women love to play, and this should be used.

10.13837. Online gaming addiction.

We should talk about female scenario dependence. Since childhood, girls play with dolls and become dependent on the plots of these games. Every girl associates herself with a doll and dreams of playing a major role.

10.13847. The desire for sex is the desire for possession.

Sex as a sublimation of lust for power. A woman wants sex over the man she wants to dominate. If a woman already has power over a man, or if he does not admire her, then there is no need to desire him.

10.13890. Vessel of evil.

A woman is a vessel of sin, but a man is what this vessel fills. A man is a proud Genie who was locked in a vessel to save the world from evil. Moreover, a woman, controlling a demon with her love, motivates him sometimes to do a useful thing. However, these two are worth each other.

10.13908.

A woman is a vessel of evil in which the demon of evil man lives. Moreover, if there is love in a woman, the whole structure turns into a Paradise house, and if there is no love, then hell comes.

10.13924. Lost love.

A proud man craves power over his woman, who sublimates into lust and desire for pleasure. Getting used to this pleasure, a man becomes a dependent drug addict, and a woman becomes a drug dealer of love. The biological programs built into a woman's brain are such that she automatically begins to restrict such a man's sex and pleasure, because drug dealers do not use their own drugs. If the program doesn't work, then the man will get an overdose of pleasure and the passion in him will die.

10.13933.

If a woman loses her fear of losing her man, she will also lose her sexual interest in him. For sex for women is an instrument of power. Especially harmful for sex is disappointment in a man, loss of understanding of his value, the idea that he is not needed by anyone and will not go anywhere.

10.13934.

For a woman in the style of chaos, sex should always be unexpected and spontaneous. Sex on a schedule or plan drives such a woman into boredom, killing passion.

10.13951.

Theoretically, the real pride of a man and the illusory pride of a woman are quite compatible.

10.13959.

Women's pride and lust for power is a setup. A woman obsessed with pride automatically feels lust, which she interprets as love, as soon as she finds a man over whom she can dominate.

10.13978.

As soon as a woman feels power, she also feels lust. Only when a man senses lust does he feel power.

10.13988.

You see, if you are a Queen, it is not for you to fight for men, but for them to fight for you. Of course, you can also choose your hero, but then you need to know what their heroes are. The hero is honest, courageous, great in his goals, not a slave to Vice. The slave of Vice is not a hero, but a coward and a weak man. By the way, lust and idolatry are also a Vice.

10.13992. Contradiction.

A proud woman, on the one hand, wants to dominate, and on the other hand, to admire the object of her passion.

10.13995. The master and Margarita.

Marguerite did not love the Master; Marguerite loved to be near the one who created. Marguerite felt the joy of being close to the creation. Margarita is a woman, she likes the process of creation. Creation is sex. Creation is a passion. A master is one who creates beauty, creates order, and creates truth.

10.13999. Vessel of sin.

A woman, wanting power over things, can sublimate the idea of all the things that a man owns in the warmth of the lower abdomen, in sex, in passion, in lust... Through sex, a woman dominates a man and all that he has and can potentially have. A man is the Lord of the world, and a woman is the Lord of a man. A man who wants to dominate a woman is like a gin who has become the slave of a jug.

10.14006.

Pride condemns women for being alone. She can't stand those who try to dominate her. She despises those over whom she was able to dominate.

10.14011. Mask of a hero and the mask of the victim.

Woman is the vessel of sin in the sense that men's pride excites their lust. A woman feels power over men's vices and this intoxicating sense of power excites her. Male pride can wear different masks. But once a woman feels it, the lustful heat in the lower abdomen drives her sinful soul crazy.

10.14022.

A woman, inflamed with passion for a pathetic man, thinks that she will be able to give him strength. But this is a lie. In fact, sensing weakness, a woman craves power, wants to take a dominant position, automatically puts a man in a passive position, further aggravating the slavery of his vices and powerlessness.

10.14118. Immune cell.

In order for a woman to dominate a man, a man needs at least some kind of Vice. Women's pride sublimates into lust and lust for sex. A woman is inexorably drawn to male vices in order to rule through them. However, the true meaning of this phenomenon is that a woman is an immune cell of being, whose task is to tame the Vice and lock the gin in a jug.

10.14119.

Women can be metaphorically called the immune cells of being, which are responsible for fighting viruses, bacteria, and diseased cells. It can also be assumed that the immune system contains information about the RNA of cells. It is the RNA that determines which DNA will be used by the stem cell to find its place in life.

10.14121.

A woman is an immune cell that studies (by loving) a man (a virus, a bacterium, or a fungus) in order to comprehend his DNA, then defeat him with his own weapon, making him a useful member of society. It is the woman who determines the role of her man in the structure of being.

10.14173.

Women get used to drug addiction faster than men, because their sensitivity is higher, but they also get off the needle faster.

10.14176.

Women's specific programs are related to their purpose in life. A woman is 98% dependent on her man. Tell me who your wife is and I'll tell you who you are.

10.14231.

Intuitively, a person loves justice and is therefore drawn to evil. The fact is that evil does not exist, evil is a lie that is very lacking in love. On the contrary, we too often turn into a false idol that overshadows the sky.

10.14245. Paranoid desire for freedom.

A female dominant personality wants a man who can be admired, but such a dominant male will subdue her and plunge her into fear.

10.14282. The skill of the druid.

A woman, of course, can be guided when choosing a man by her intuition and joy, but it should be remembered that biologically a woman likes two types of men. The first she is ready to admire and serve them, and over the vices of the second she wants to rule. The lust for power is pride that makes life hell. Proud women automatically fall in love with very vicious men or are doomed to live alone. When a proud woman sees a vicious man, it seems to her that if she gives him love, he will grow up. But, alas, the fruitless Fig tree does not always begin to bear fruit.

10.14283.

A woman's pride makes her search for darkness and try to turn it into light. In this positive desire, the main thing is to realize that pleasure is not the main thing here, because if a woman becomes fixated on pleasure and her own heroism, she will lose interest in the light. Such people like to feel sorry for and help, but they don't like those who are doing well.

10.14284.

The help woman loves those who need help. But when she pulls a man out of the mud and washes him, her sexual interest will instantly disappear, because it was not the man she loved, but the dirt.

10.14286. Contrasting background.

The problem with women who want to turn darkness into light is that they don't know how to do it. Theoretically, when you yourself have too much fear and ignorance, a minus on a minus should give a plus, but in practice, women just get pleasure from other people's minuses, against which their minuses turn into pluses.

10.14289.

A woman inside herself should be black and accept this blackness. A woman is a witch admiring the light of angels. Women's task: to motivate men to become white angels with their admiration.

10.14290. "I'm good" is nice.

A woman who is focused on her whiteness (goodness) will subconsciously look for a darker man to create a contrasting spiritual background. Such a woman will find vicious men and subconsciously preserve them in this state. At the same time, if such a man gets rid of his vices, she will leave him.

10.14291.

A woman who considers herself perfect needs a very imperfect man to create a contrasting background and revel in her own greatness. And the worse such a man is, the happier such a woman is. To be able to love a normal man, such a woman should accept her dark half.

10.14307.

She seems strong to herself because she has fallen out of love and suffered. All emotions, including the fear in her, became very quiet. Alas, this is just armor, under which a very gentle, devoid of any immunity, soul.

10.14336. Man test.

All the female traits that usually infuriate men are just intuitive ways to experience a man. A woman checks whether this man has patience, courage, wisdom, and love.

10.14354. A stupid desire.

Do you want to be a Princess?
"What a fool! You foolishly envy the princesses, not knowing that the pea is a hellish curse of any Princess, from which you can not get rid of.

10.14357.

There must be a mystery in a woman, and in a man, too. Love is the experience of knowledge, and when you have exhausted the object of knowledge, you will also exhaust love.

10.14369. Murderers of love.

To sum up, it is not necessary to turn a woman (or a man) into your source of pleasure and then she (he) will not run away. A woman is not a drug. A man's desire to make a drug out of a woman turns a man into a drug addict, and a woman into a cold and cynical drug dealer. Drug dealers don't use drugs, so a love dealer can't love.

10.14372.

Princess Nesmeyana is so sad that the princes have tired her with their exploits and gifts. Too many positive emotions turned her life into hell.

10.14398.

Usually a woman leaves her man in two cases. First, he ceases to see it as the source of his joy. Second, it becomes his only source of joy.

10.14447.

A massive attack of male love plunges a woman into despair, and she gives up. Women's despair they call love.

10.14452.

Women are powerless before what they feel, but they can easily kill old feelings with new feelings.

10.14457.

No wonder a man thinks that you can fall in love with a woman, satiating her with travel, luxury and pleasure. The torment of the Princess on the pea is terrible. Princess Nesmeyana truly hates her tormentors.

10.14479.

When love dies in a woman who was an idol, she looks for something pathetic and weak, devoid of pride, to give it energy. The former idolater held sway over her. Automatically, a woman like that needs someone weak to control.

10.14518.

It's easier to maintain a relationship with a woman than to restore it later. However, given the pride and ignorance of men, they usually prefer the hard way.

10.14521. Predatory Flycatcher.

A woman can give a man energy, but usually she does it to lure a Genie into a magic lamp. All further activities of the woman are reduced to sabotage and diverting the energy of the Genie from its true goals. In fact, gin, now works not for himself, but for the lamp.

10.14542.

It is a mistake to think that women need a long sexual act. First, women are different, and secondly, the average person has enough sex once or twice a week, about 15-20 minutes, and everything else is exhausting. The error of men is extreme. They turn sex into half a minute, then a marathon and some kind of theatrical show. All this causes chronic frustration in women.

10.14554. Sadness in the eyes.

A man who focuses on power over a woman through sex is not very interesting to such a woman, because she would like to rule over him herself. It is interesting for a woman to give pleasure and joy to a man herself. If it is not possible to bring joy to a man, she suffers greatly, this reduces her self-esteem and self-confidence. A woman intuitively feels that in a person who has no joy, there is no love.

10.14576.

False love breeds fear. Fear begins to control the person. Fear is pride and lies. The woman senses lies and fear, and automatically closes.

10.14616.

There are many reasons why women live in the wilds of their illusions. There are just as many reasons why they can't be pulled out.

10.14626.

If you put emotional pressure on a woman, harass her or spoil her mood, she will emotionally close, ceasing to feel negative and positive, that is, she will become indifferent in bed.

10.14638. Imagine that the angels are protecting you.

One day in San Cristobal (Mexico), when I went out at midnight, I saw a woman who looked like a Queen surrounded by several guards with machine guns. The power of this woman's pride and power was so enormous that people were scattered in different directions from her like leaves in the autumn wind or like cards in a fairy tale about Alice.

10.14645. A righteous anger.

You don't pay attention to me – it's not called love. Your lack of love for me makes me fear that you don't love me. I could run away from fear, I could ignore it, but I love you, and so I will attack my fear. Anger is a situation where I attack my fear and want to get your attention. You don't love me, so know my anger.

10.14659.

A woman is mother earth, and a man is either the Sun or the Moon. However, the opposite is not less common.

10.14665.

It's very dangerous to ignore the woman you love.

10.14731. Lost happiness.

If a woman in the family focuses on the external, then her internal will decline, turning into a swamp or completely dry up.

10.14847.

A woman is necessary for a man who has no brains of his own. When a man doesn't have ideas that are worthy of love, a woman comes on the scene and finds something useful for him. In the absence of a woman, a man can easily morally decompose and become a slave to vices.

10.14850. Get a job!

Women's pride, the higher, the more effectively it can attract work for her beloved man. Work is a grace and a miracle, for it is a source of joy and money.

10.14901.

A man's desire to possess a woman is pride that turns a Genie into a slave to a magic lamp.

10.14933.

The ideal of a woman "Sun", a kind of eternally rejoicing sun is a purely male idealistic ideal. The proud man wants the eternal sun, but the eternal joy will turn him into a demon addict and kill him, and the sun woman will also suffer terribly. In fact, the negative can not be extinguished. You can't lie. Negativity should be turned into righteous anger and turned to the angel of order. A proud man who wants power must always be stopped by anger.

10.14950.

The image of the sun woman is an idealized male image of the ideal drug. A man who looks for a drug in a woman inevitably turns his life into a drug addict's hell.

10.14964.

Women feel a man's greedy hunger and thirst for power. If a woman feels a man's pride, she runs away from him in terror. Don't turn a woman into a source of pleasure, don't try to eat her, and women will be attracted to you.

10.14965.

It's not that women don't like smart men, but women don't like chatty whiners and demagogues. Women love hands and hard-working men. A man who can and loves to work is an object of increased sexual passion for a woman.

10.14966. You need to take care of yourself.

A man tries to dominate hard, belittling women's self-esteem. A woman should respond to such an attempt at power with righteous anger and send it to hell. If a woman doesn't say any-thing, anxiety will sublimate into guilt and fear. In General, all this is stressful and harmful to health. A man should behave similarly.

10.14976.

Fear makes people greedy. The more cowardly a woman is, the more she will eat her man's brain for his income. The more beautiful a woman is, the more fear there is in her, for the fear of losing her beauty fills her whole life with fear.

10.14985. The vessel of evil is the Keeper of fire.

A woman is a vessel of evil, but not evil itself. Evil is a man, and a woman, depending on her experience and perfection, can turn this evil into light. A man is an oil with a wick that can be poured into a vessel, set on fire and then it will turn into a can-dle that gives light. The meaning of a woman, as a vessel of fire, is to store and feed the fire, keeping it alive, while not allowing it to turn into an all-consuming fire.

10.15008. Scenario # 14.

As a child, my father and daughter watched a movie and my father, seeing a joyful and dancing female character, said that this should be a real woman. The daughter heard this and decided to become the embodiment of her father's dream of an ideal female idol. The girl was young and stupid, and her father wasn't far from her either. They didn't know how to distinguish the illusion of a movie from real life. In reality, it is impossible to be happy forever, for this you will have to close yourself from reality and hide in the world of your illusions, create your own movie, which the girl did. Then she found a husband who, admiring a beautiful idol, loved her very much... and became addicted to her drug addict. You know what drug addicts are like, right? Pride and lust for power are all of them. Lust, lust for pleasure, trying to get a new dose at any cost. As a result, the idolater gave the idol gifts, overfed her so that she was forced to close off from him emotionally. Closing off the negative and overdose of emotions, the girl stopped enjoying sex and intimacy with her husband. YOU know these idolatrous men, they are so touchy, any hint of a lack of love drives them mad. In General, in this happy fairy tale, everyone died and went to hell, where they lived for an eternity very unhappily and sadly.

10.15025. Unhealthy love.

It so happens that the male crushes and puts pressure on the woman until she breaks and can't accept. Theoretically, humility is also love, but it is a kind of dull love, not at all joyful. On the other hand, it happens that, resigned, a woman feels the joy of relief, and becomes dependent on this joy. Having got used to such love, the woman begins to act similarly in relation to the man.

10.15032. There are devils in a quiet pool.

A cowardly man, wanting to take over a woman, chooses the quietest and most modest, in the hope that she is the weakest. The problem is that the less, the more. The one who is looking for a slave, he becomes slave.

10.15035.

They say women love with their ears. This is because increased sensitivity allows them not only to see, but also to hear and feel. Men love with their eyes from their initially reduced sensitivity, when the sense of vision begins to prevail. However, after falling in love, a man ceases to see, and only hears what a woman says in his ear or yells loudly.

10.15043. Whatever you choose, it won't change anything.

A man, choosing a quiet and modest girl, should always remember that there are devils in a quiet pool. On the other hand, a passionate lioness will also eat you, so there is nothing to choose from.

10.15046.

A woman in her bad desire to be good spoils everything. Against the background of a man who is an order, she feels a drop in self-esteem, that I am bad. To save yourself, you should say to yourself "Yes, I'm bad" and rejoice in this. However, a man in such a situation should behave the same way.

10.15048.

When the husband is too good and strong, the wife automatically falls into fear, laziness and procrastination in order to fix the dominant-dependent relationship. Nature is so specially made that a woman avoids the temptation to destroy the family.

10.15050. You can't be so bad.

A woman may admire her man, but the emotional defense

mechanism will reject him. He is so good and loves me, and I am so bad... the Feeling of "I am bad" will turn on the feeling of love and close all emotions, as a result, sexual desire and love in a woman will disappear, and their place will be taken by fear and doubt.

10.15061.

Your problem is that you are a witch, but you are trying to deny your nature. You want to be good, but I tell you truly, you are good when you are bad.

10.15062. Inner voice.

They tell you you're bad. Don't believe it. You're good because you're bad. Your standard is the standard of chaos. Those who love you want to dominate you and therefore try to impose their standards on you. If you try to follow their standards, you fall into an abyss of misery. I don't love you and I don't want power over you, so trust me and be what your inner voice requires you to be.

10.15077.

The philosophy of Syntalism will be especially useful for women who suffer from the despotism and pride of men.

10.15081.

The situation when a woman does not work, does not work enough and has too much rest and entertainment, generates exhaustion of the nervous system, acute neurosis and depression.

10.15104.

If you feel bad, people close to you tell you that you are bad, and it hurts you... You want to get rid of the pain, but for some reason it doesn't work... Do you know why? Because it's impossible. You are chaos! You're a witch! You must agree with your nature! You have to say, " Yes, I'm bad and that's my strength-

!"And rejoice in it.

10.15494. Passionately in love.

Women are persistent in their desires. Women know how to love better than men. Love is perseverance, knowledge, care, and patience. Everything a woman wants to do, she will do, break her head, and do...

10.16084.

A woman who did well in school can be a problem wife, because her overflowing idealism, tightness and desire to control everything can turn any family into hell.

10.16125.

An evil wife is an ignorant and cowardly wife. However, as a wife, so is a husband.

10.16372. The first law of love.

When a woman believes that she is truly loved, she automatically falls in love with the answer. However, if a woman feels that this is false love, pride and narcissism, then there will be no reciprocal love. However, women's love has the same power over men. Nothing can resist true love

10.16571.

Women love with their ears, because their imagination knows no limit. Women like to dream. Fantasy perfectly magnifies words, turning them into huge dreams.

10.16728.

A witch needs a normal Mature demon, and there are no such ones, there are only devils youngsters. To turn the imp into a demon, you need to beat it and torture it. Growing up is through pain and experience.

10.16730.

Only after sensing a man's desire for power and restraint, the witch rushes to him to rule.

10.16743.

A woman's problem is that she wants power over a man, but she doesn't understand that she needs a man she can't beat, but she can sometimes win and partially restrain.

10.16748.

A woman goes wild when she feels a Vice in men and children.

10.16760.

It is very useful for a woman to communicate with smart men, the society of weak and intelligent men negatively affects women's character and health.

10.16763.

To a weak and stupid man, a woman is dangerous. Stupidity and immaturity will breed pride and a thirst for power. If a weak man tries to possess a woman, he will instantly turn her into a witch and become her slave.

10.16847.

There is nothing worse than a woman who encourages a man to love himself. The goal of a woman is to encourage a man to high goals of reason, and she who inclines a man to idolatry is called a witch.

10.17318.

Gene is asleep. Gene is sick, he has no soul, there is no love in him. Sleep saves from pain, sleep heals. They say you can dream about love. They say a sleeping beauty waits to be woken by a kiss.

10.17329.

A woman always reflects her man honestly. A man who is dissatisfied with his woman is a liar and a proud man, unable to accept himself as he is. In fact, it is an inferiority complex, compensated by narcissism.

10.17330.

A woman is the books she has read and the men she has slept with

10.17444.

Noble, proud, haughty... This is what beauty and power look like.

10.17461.

Desires cause suffering, but the absence of desires is painful. Therefore, women, without knowing what they want, prefer men who tell them their desires.

10.17465.

Try to please a woman, but don't try to suppress her and teach her.

10.17474.

After the birth of a child, a woman usually loses sexual interest in her man, because for thousands of years of human history, after giving birth to children, a man went in search of truth, money, or war. As a rule, a woman raised children on her own.

10.18112.

A woman should love a man by admiring what he does. Admires the process of work, and only through it is beautiful tool. Admires the anticipation of a beautiful result. Women really like the process of pregnancy.

10.18136.

When a woman witch feels a proud man who wants to make an idol of her, on the level of instincts, she feels that the more you fight with him, the more he will love her. It's all about pride, if you don't belittle a proud man, he will become proud and stop loving you. Women's intuition knows this. A man who wants to escape from a witch needs to control his pride on his own.

10.18141.

It's not a good idea to buy a woman gifts without her. However, men also do not really like unnecessary things.

10.18162.

The witch is infuriated by fear. When a witch feels fear, she turns violent in disgust.

10.18163.

The witch herself is a coward, so the fear of others is unbearable to her.

10.18167.

A woman says to a man: "You can't hear me." He answers: "Men love with their eyes, please write me your wish."

10.18173.

A proud woman can have the following relationship options... a Weak alcoholic. A strong tyrant. Patronizing order(with such unbearably boring). Someone who tolerates her, but she despises him. Maybe the one who runs away will leave her alone.

10.18188.

Sensing fear, the witch goes mad with lust for power.

10.18204. Mathematical abstraction.

A woman is a reflection of a man, but a mirror is magic... Others call it a crooked mirror, but it's not like that. Algorithms by which the mirror of a woman's soul reflects a man should be described using nonlinear differential equations.

10.18248.

A woman is a mirror of a man. Yes, this mirror can be crooked, hypertrophied or magical, ... but still a lot depends on the man.

10.18272. Get to know me.

A woman needs love. She feels that love is knowledge and patience. And a selfish, proud man doesn't want to know her. Without knowing a woman, a man cannot guess her desires. A man tries to somehow save the relationship, gives some gifts, but everything is not in the subject and everything is not the same. This indicates that he is inattentive and narcissistic. In this situation, the woman intuitively begins to provoke scandals or coldly ignore the man. A woman wants conflict, because war, like love, is a great way to know your enemy.

10.18276. Female neuroticism.

The main problem of modern women is the cowardice of men. Cowards can't love. Faced with love, a coward man runs away, this sublimates into divorce, alcoholism, infidelity and other vices. The second reaction to fear is aggression, cowards begin to brawl, some even beat a woman. It is very difficult to find an adequate manly man who can solve problems calmly and with a sense of humor.

10.18280. Life is love.

As long as a woman fights with a man, she loves him. Indifference is the death of love. A scandal is a neurotic conflict, a means of attracting attention. Just as the Moon warms up the magma inside the Earth and provokes the tides, a woman's scandals warm up love in a man's heart. The moon generates volcanic activity on Earth that creates the atmosphere and warms the water. The moon is the cause of life on Earth.

10.18292. A man needs a man.

A woman's problem is that she can't find a man. The fire of love is burning in a woman. Midges fly to the fire, and the midges burn in it. Proud nocturnal predators they walk in circles, but do not want to approach, looking with hungry eyes out of the night. Animals do not want and do not know how to love. A woman needs a normal reasonable person. A person who can admire fire and knows a lot about it. A person who will feed the fire and take care of it. A man who is brave and smart enough not to be afraid of fire. A man who is not afraid to love himself and fire at the same time.

10.18345.

Proud women are doomed to love the slaves of Vice. Pride craves power, love cannot be owned... The slaves remain.

10.18363.

Women are social to the core. What does she want from her man? Envy your friends!

10.18383.

Metaphorically, a man is the Earth, which is required to be fruitful, and a woman is the Moon. The point is that a man should love the sun, that is, his dream, then a woman will love her man for his fruitfulness and life. The situation where a man instead of love and work focuses on volcanic activity associated with power over the Moon makes sense only in the early stages of the history of the planet Earth.

10.18385.

By metaphorically imagining a woman as fire, you will learn to treat both women and love. Everything depends on you. Feed the fire, keep your hands off it, restrain its greed... and enjoy its warmth... What could be simpler? If you imagine a man as a fire

– it will not change anything fundamentally.

10.18809.

When a woman has a child, she finds love and loses fear of her man. And after all, she did not particularly love a man, they were bound by fear, for example, the fear of loneliness. Having lost fear, a woman comes into conflict with a man.

10.18810.

Often a woman falls in love with a man out of fear of loneliness. In this case, after the birth of the child, when there is love for the child, against the background of love, fear disappears and the woman loses interest in the man.

10.18811.

A woman who has lived with a man for a certain number of years takes over his qualities, and becomes very similar to him. In this situation, the domineering man should be careful, and also need to know the woman, taking part of her softness. If this is not done, the relationship will fall apart.

10.18814.

At best, until the age of 33, a woman is willing to tolerate a man's claim to power, after which she learns enough from men to become like them and challenge power. In the future, building a relationship based on fear will not work and you will have to switch to love and mutual respect.

10.18826.

A woman is looking for someone who will love her for who she is. This is quite real, but requires mutual tolerance.

10.18973.

A dependent woman in fear of losing her man will keep him by limiting sex and being painful. Feeling inattentive and unfaithful, she will also try to provoke scandals and guilt.

10.18987.

The fire woman needs a water man who can be safely boiled. The man is the ocean, and the woman is the moon, which causes the tides in it.

10.18993.

Venus is a symbol of female consciousness removed from love and from this gone mad.

10.18995.

When a woman is fire or water, a man must show the firmness and restraint of a stone.

10.19001.

Woman with the syndrome Cleopatra will constantly try to attract attention and feels the lack of love. When her joys are exhausted, she will crave rest in order to restore her sensitivity to pleasure.

10.19009. The best defense is a good offense.

Cleopatra (idol) complex) there is a consequence of over-love, narcissistic personality disorder, in essence, drug addiction. Drug addicts are unhappy people, and their favorite defense strategy is to attack. Because addicts are afraid of everything in the world, they are very aggressive, touchy and nervous.

10.19024.

Women like verbs, women like action and process, and women don't really believe words. In this respect, life is very similar to a woman.

10.19042.

A woman craves power and high self-esteem, making it her

source of energy. A proud, power-hungry woman is very profitable for an alcoholic man (any kind of addiction), because the angel feels especially good against the background of a demon. Subconsciously, a woman with her criticism and contempt lowers the self-esteem of this man, further preserving him in the power of the drug.

10.19089. Sluggish sex.

A woman in a passive-dependent relationship always reduced sexual activity. Chronic anxiety and fears reduce emotional sensitivity, including sexual sensitivity.

10.19090.

The dominant man will experience sexual insufficiency, and the woman will constantly restrain him.

10.19105.

Chronic fear, reduces sensitivity and sexual activity. Women whose heads are full of patterns and stereotypes are constantly afraid of their violations, which greatly reduces their sexuality.

10.19108.

For a woman with low sexual activity, it makes sense to stop pestering and give her a chance to take an active position. Activity can bring it to life.

10.19219.

When a woman hears a lie, she feels discomfort that is very similar to pain. A woman's ability to feel a lie is the fear of pain.

10.19235.

Men's talk about their own unworthiness does not frighten women, because they like to rule and feel like heroines.

10.19242. Suicide.

The proud man makes all his pleasure a part of his one Ego. A woman creates a sub-personality for every pleasure, and when love dies, she kills this sub-personality.

10.19246.

The wife of a dominant man of pride will calmly treat his problems at work. The wife benefits from the fall in the level of power and complacency of the husband.

10.19303.

Men's pride is great, but women's pride is even greater. The power struggle between women is uncompromising.

10.19323.

Usually the energy runs after a beautiful form, begging it to rule over itself.

10.19344.

The cat and its 9 lives is a classic symbol of a woman. The female personality is a conglomerate of subpersonalities.

10.19359.

A woman herself will know a man and will strive for unity with him if she admires him, and a man will show restraint and not try to enslave her.

10.19382.

Women cling to men who are proud, because they are dependent on pleasure, and therefore they can be controlled either by pleasure or by fear.

10.19386.

A woman is very sensitive to the falseness of a man, because the lie is sublimated into fear and, multiplying with the native female fear, turns into suspiciousness.

10.19388.

A woman attracts a man either with love (admiration and joy), or with fear when there is no love. When there is no love, a woman attracts a man's attention with conflicts and fears.

10.19410. Three women's ideas.

He doesn't understand me. He must. It will change. However, not only women's.

10.19428.

Women are extremely negative and fearful of men's vices. The slave of vices loves only his own Vice, and therefore does not love a woman. Feeling the lack of self-love, a woman experiences fear and anger. Fear greatly reduces a woman's mood and sexual attraction to a man.

10.19466.

A woman needs to be given attention, but she doesn't need to be given power. And you can't spoil them with gifts.

10.19472.

Big and bright love is after all pride, which is quickly satiated. Women who demand great and passionate love are doomed to suffer. Or they themselves will get fed up with this attention, and they will begin to despise such a man. Or the man will get fed up with her attention and run away to look for novelty in other places.

10.19476. I am fire.

A woman is a metaphor for love. God is love, love is perfection. Love is tenderness, care, attention and fire. The fire should keep you warm. Fire should not burn or cause pain. The aggressiveness of the fire is pride.

10.19477. The immutable law.

The evolution of similar systems is the same. The laws of evolution are a constant. A woman always chooses the same type of man, because she does not change. She constantly chooses A, which grows and evolves into B, but she does not like B and again chooses A. the Circle closes. However, men who are hungry for love, think similarly.

10.19479.

The problem with a woman is that when she tries to keep a man's attention on her, she Sates him and pushes him away from her. A woman should be a fire and warm. The fire, of course, needs to be fed, but the idea that someone likes to live in a fire is doubtful. A man can return to the fire, where there is peace and warmth, but the moths fly to the fire and burn.

10.19480. Fire requires humility.

Female fire, of course, attracts moths, but moths in the fire quickly burn up and disappear forever. Predators also look at the fire with curiosity, but sensibly avoid it. Fire needs a reasonable person who will show restraint and care about fire. You can't overfeed the fire, you can't climb into it with your face and body, but you need to take it lightly feed.

10.19481. The symbol of the burning Kupava is a symbol of humility in love.

The greedy thirst for love is the desire for fire, so that the moths fly into the fire. Fire requires sacrifices in the form of burning, which is stupid. The fire thinks it can get enough of the moths, but it won't. The moths are very small and burn quickly. The fire lives in perpetual fear that it may go out. The truth is that fire does not need moths, which fire despises, or animals that fear it, but a reasonable person who knows how to handle fire.

10.19489.

The female idea that "I should be won over" is pride and manipulation. True love is eternal fire. What does it matter to him whether the wolf came to warm himself or not?

10.19505.

A woman is love, love is a flower that rejoices in the rain, heat and sun. A man is a bee. Of course, a bee may be addicted to a particular flower and be jealous of other bees, but the flower's suffering is stupid. The idea of a flower-to put a bee on a chain-seems very strange to us.

10.19511.

A woman tries to control a man with her passion. A man who is dependent on women's love is doomed to communicate with women who will try to actively dominate him.

10.19512.

A good man is worth his weight in gold, and women are ready to bite their throats out for such a man to each other and to him. This creates jealousy, a desire to control it, guilt, and fear.

10.19523.

The male Creator is imperfect, he still needs to grow and train. Woman perfect from the very beginning and ready to create a person.

10.19534.

A woman is a metaphor for the world and its environment, a symbol of the thirst for power and control. Man is the symbol of unity, the symbol of growth. Zero is harmoniously tending to one. The more zeros a unit has, the stronger it is.

10.19535.

Cowardly and amorous women are extremely jealous and aggressive, trying to control everything and instill a sense of guilt in their men. Including a man in their self-esteem, they are terribly afraid of losing him, invent some ideals for themselves and try to adjust a man to this ideal. These women deliberately take a passive position with the dominant man in order to manipulate him, instilling a sense of guilt or inferiority complex.

10.19554.

There are always three women. YOU who are... You are what you would like to be and could be. And you, who you were. Remember, you are a perfect non-Copernicus, and you are past no longer fit for reality. Even if your man he'll run off to one of these two women, and if you're calm and steady, he'll be back soon.

10.19560. The fair maiden.

You are ashamed, you blush... the Words " red» and "beautiful" are similar in Russian. Your embarrassment and shame make you beautiful.

10.19562.

A woman always feels more than a man, because she includes the whole man in her self-esteem.

10.19563.

Women's greedy pride craves growth and fruitfulness. It is assumed that a man in love, having got rid of fear, acquires courage and the ability to grow. If growth does not occur, but instead there is fear, alcoholism and other vices, this causes a woman to rage.

10.19567.

Every woman has an angel and a demon in her. Love me black means that initially you communicated with an angel, the light side of a woman, ... but love is everything. Love to ride, love to drive a sled. So learn to negotiate and communicate with the demon. Especially in the man is also living angels and demons.

It takes two devils to come to terms with each other.

10.19570. The whip and the carrot.

A woman wants her man to grow. The angels love, when life grows. When there is no growth, a demon with a whip wakes up in a woman. The task of the demon: fire and sword to awaken the craving for life in a man.

10.19573.

Of course, a woman she can also independently realize her pride through her career, but she likes to do it through her man more.

10.19581.

The family can be seen as a nuclear reactor, where the man is nuclear fuel, and women are the control rods. Women's task: to heat up the system, generating a chain reaction, while simultaneously holding it back from explosion and avalanche-like disintegration. This state of Affairs directs a woman to order, and a man to explosive expansion and fruitful growth. The woman's task is to make sure that the system performs useful work, and there are no energy leaks.

10.19589.

A woman who lowers a man's self-esteem with her reproaches creates in him a feeling of insufficiency and a desire to grow. A woman does the same with children. And the woman will do it either with love or with fear.

10.19590.

Pride is the pleasure and the lust for power. If a woman feels a lack of pleasure and attention, she will satisfy her thirst pleasure through the desire for power and control.

10.19671.

Beautiful people are hungry for power and have a chronic fear of not having enough power. Beautiful women are hard to love, they never get enough attention, they want to attract attention... and this, of course, turns them into nervous and love-dependent drug addicts.

10.19717.

I was abandoned, so I'm bad. It hurts... The subconscious switches from complex mode to narcissism. I'm perfect, he's not worthy of me.

10.19727.

Passive wife drips order on the brain, drips, ... he swears, but listens, but slowly does.

10.19829.

People need attention, if they are left without attention, people suffer greatly.

10.19831.

A woman wants power over a man, but if she wins, she will despise him. A woman needs a man to admire. You can't admire and love someone you control.

10.19880. A woman is water.

I have noticed that in a relationship, the more a man holds back a woman's love, the more a woman loves him. Moreover, this deterrence can be even the most aggressive and boorish.

10.19929.

Classic female consciousness is the consciousness of a drug addict, dependent on love and attention, who goes out of his way to get another dose of the drug. Moreover, an overdose of love generates a strong addiction and withdrawal. However, a man in this matter is no different from a woman.

10.19958.

A woman intuitively prefers to swear with a man when she feels problems, believing that a strong and intelligent man will try to fulfill the commandment "Love your enemy" and, having known the problem, will solve all the issues.

10.19978.

Women who are dependent on beauty are dependent on attention. They want to be the center of attention, and when they lose that attention, they go wild.

10.19980.

Her mother told her to" chain Up, " and she ran away and got into trouble... Then went back on the chain. Now the same thing that mother did to her, she did with her husband. She tells her husband: "Sit on the circuit" and he runs off and comes back broken. She is angry and waiting for repentance.

10.20015.

You've been taught love all your life... First by your mother, who didn't know how to love herself, then by your husband, who is hardly a role model. There were also some friends and strange books. In the end, your whole life is suffering, and you still don't know how to love.

10.20058.

The main thing is calm. Refuse a woman without anger or aggression. Anger is not necessary. Do what you think is best, but without anger.

10.20063. A sense of fear.

Women often develop paranoia when they feel that their husband is cheating on them.

10.20078.

When a woman rages and is not in the mood, do not argue with her and show your anger, you need to wait out the storm. Speak, I understand. Feel sorry for her, keep your distance.

10.20104.

The more cowardly and suspicious a woman is, the more insensitive and courageous a man she chooses to save her from fear... All my life then this woman tries to remake it, and suffers that it is bad.

10.20115.

Men whose souls are filled with pride and narcissism are doomed to have big problems in the family, their wives will always be sick, and give them a lot of problems. As for children, there will be no special joy from children. However, proud and narcissistic women are not very happy either.

10.20130.

The frog Princess is an excellent metaphor that reveals the contrasting essence of a certain type of woman. In one way it is beautiful, and in another it is disgusting.

10.20166.

Women understand the feeling of power as love.

10.20405.

There are different ways to restrain love. You can be scandals and conflicts, you can lower someone else's self-esteem, you can pretend to be a Princess Not funny, but you can arrange a quiet sabotage ... and constantly slip away.

10.20742. The kettle is on fire.

Woman is the energy and fire of pride, and man is the fertility of water, protected from fire by firmness.

10.20974.

Script "love me black» allows a woman to understand whether her man has at least a little bit of real love, which is characterized by patience, courage, wisdom and calm.

10.21235. Flirting with the family.

A woman lacks signs of attention and displays of feelings. A woman likes to hear phrases like: I missed you, how good you are, how good you are, glad to see you, etc.

10.21259.

A woman pursuing a man is inclined to use psychological violence, trying to attract his attention in any way, to manipulate feelings of guilt, pity and sexuality.

10.21384.

The more order a woman has, the more attention she demands. The procedure requires admiration to your address and tries to structure chaos. In response to admiration in its address, order will love chaos, and transfer its energy to it.

10.21386.

A woman who is afraid wants to find a man who can be filled with her fears and who can save her. Men do not need to complain much to women, because women have enough of their own fears. It is assumed that a man who falls in love with a woman will lose fear and become masculine. At the same time, a woman, feeling the courage of a man, will fall in love with him.

10.21613.

A woman who believes in her husband delegates her faith to him, thus doubling his strength. Faith is a movement. The wife is happy when the husband makes a move towards their shared hopes and dreams. If the wife feels that the movement has stopped, she is overcome with fear and very bad mood. A lazy man turns a woman into a witch.

10.22004.

Women intuitively gather for a long time to make their men wait. Love is patient. False love is pride, very impatient and aggressive. Pride must be subdued in order to turn it into love.

10.22006.

When a man is proud and greedy for pleasure, he seeks sex from his woman, and the woman restricts his access to sex, she thus subdues pride and turns it into love.

10.22542.

A woman needs a man who can save her from herself.

10.22543.

A woman doesn't know what she wants. Cats on her soul they argue furiously with each other, giving rise to headaches. You can support any cat and create a balance of forces in your side.

10.22605.

A man with vices is very useful for a woman to self-justify her own vices and raise her self-esteem.

10.22615.

I know you're not who you pretend to be... I see the real you.

10.22631.

Proud women like cowardly men, they like to rule. On the other hand, pride is a source of great suffering.

AFTERWORD

10.22334. A grain of sand.

Variothoughts is sand, not gold. According to Syntalism, our world is built of sand, not gold. The most valuable thing is sand, sand is bread, and gold is salt.

10.22742.

Variothoughts books should be read slowly, chewing every thought carefully. Truth is that which has extension properties, and falsehood is pride, that is, an avid rush.

10.22339.

There are no questions that cannot be answered in the Variothoughts. The Variothoughts is an endless source of inspiration for hearts searching for truth.

10.22266. Nutcracker.

Breaking stereotypes and patterns. Variothoughts is a brain-crushing book, the meaning of which is to achieve the integrity of the mind. First, all beliefs should be destroyed in the dust, and then it will all stick together and enlightenment will come.

10.22554. The living and the dead book.

In the original, Variothoughts is the ideal of the perfection of truth, but the ideal is dead and, therefore, there is no joy in it. To bring back the joy of life to Variothoughts, I decided to salt the bread. Salt-free bread is too sweet. In Variothoughts transla-tions, I threw a couple of spoons of chaos. My act of monstrous vandalism led to the loss of 20% of the meaning, and made the texts very strange and obscure. You will call me a scoundrel and a vandal, but I don't think so ... On the contrary, I believe it made the texts charming, created artificial barriers ... Now, to understand the texts of Variothoughts and find the truth, you have to smash your head and think. Thinking is joyful.

10.15530.

The basis of speech is truth. Cognition of truth should begin with clarifying the meaning of words.

10.16833.

The main feature of Variothoughts is its unprecedented honesty. No censorship of thoughts, absolute freedom of ideas and words.

5.412.

Variothoughts is a book for those who save their time. Ready-made Lego cubes used to put together any ideas and goals. The DNA and RNA of thought.

3.2212. Attainment of truth.

A comprehensive attainment of reality occurs by knowledge's thinning of its tiniest degree of detail.

3.2213.

Unity is hidden in differences. You unite by disuniting. Holding one onto another, the infinitely small becomes the infinitely big.

10.6168.

The Variothoughts is a basic library of DNA of thought, loading it into the brain can solve any problem. Any dreams, any goals will be available to you, thanks to the philosophy of Syntalism.

3.1971.

Variothoughts implements divergent thought algorithms in order to come again to unity through a multitude. Many grows out of one and one grows again out of many.

3.2211.

Soundness is the ability to dynamically examine things from different perspectives.

3.2216.

Having reached its limit, knowledge transforms into will. What is the limit of knowledge? – Faith.

10.21243. Love of truth.

The meaning of human life is to overcome infinite loneliness and find infinite love.

ABOUT THE AUTHOR

8.2479.

SoloINC (anc.greek "combining the uncombinable", keeper of the grain")

Soloinc Logic, philosopher from the city of Sofia. Soloinc (Diamond Solo / Solodilov Dmitry), Bulgarian psychologist and Stoic philosopher. Supporter of the merger of logical and sensory methods of cognition. He considers the connection of traditional philosophies with modern science. He is the founder of the cyberphilosophy of Syntalism (Quantum Nanophilosphy), which considers the problems of philosophy, sociology, psychology and economics in terms of systemic cybernetics and logic.

Soloinc is not the first, but the last philosopher. Evangelist and cyberpunk guru. The author of more than 73 thousand original ideas and thoughts. Main books: "Variothoughts", "Diamond Stoic", "Theory of Existence", "Money Bible", "Quantum Philosophy", "Mathematics and Progression", "Velerechie", "The Device of the Mind", "Royal Buffoon", "Liberastia" , "Surrotic", "Surfutur" and others, in total more than 888 books.

3.1753.

In fact, Variothoughts is very tedious. I have seeked the truth all my life, then I found it and concealed it in a different place. Variothoughts is an intellectual quest and a mosaic of truth, broken into thousands of pieces. I found the truth in plain sight and concealed it back as well as before… What's the point? It's a game or a way to kill boredom. We live eternally and boredom turns our life into hell. I want to save you from sufferings for some reason...

10.21128. Soloinc Music

Soloinc Music is a stunningly beautiful integrity of music and text, admiring metaphors and secret meanings. Soloinc Music is a pleasure for living minds who have dedicated their lives to the search for beauty and truth. Soloinc Music awakens the minds and ignites the heart. Everyone will find joy and strength to live in it.

10.2341. A realistic mysticism.

The genre of poetry and music of Soloinc is a mystical realism. Most Soloinc songs are mystical ballads or religious hymns, prophecies, and insights. Soloinc lyrics are always metaphors and mystical signs. They cannot be taken literally. These are grains of sand in which entire worlds are hidden. All words are the opposite. To understand the meaning of the Variothoughts texts you need to read from bottom to top, from right to left.

Syntalism - Generative Quantum Nanophilosphy

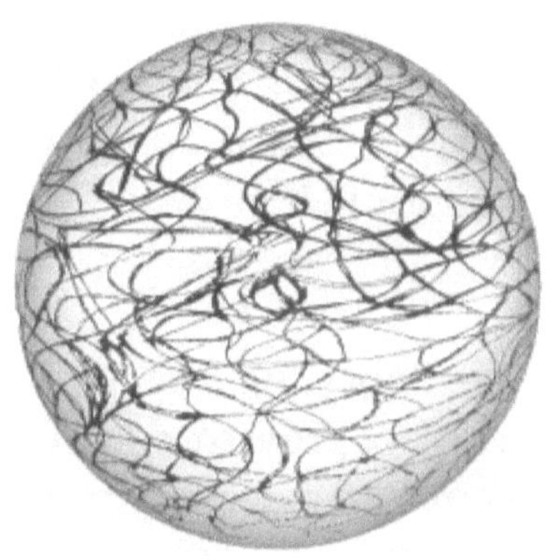 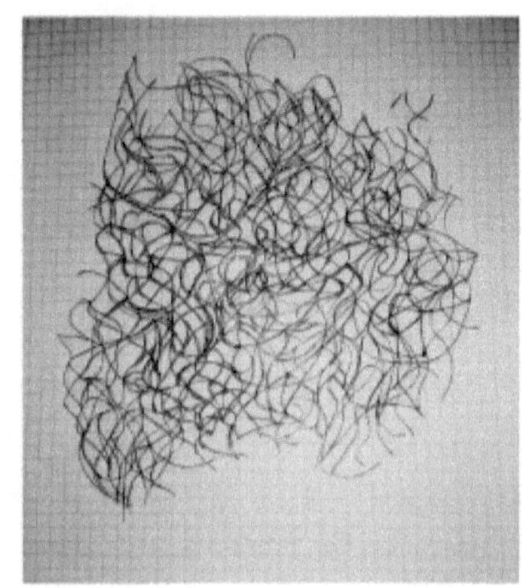

10.19296.

The philosophy of Syntalism was inspired by the poetry of life, expressed in the poems of such poets as Shakespeare, Robert Burns, Williams Blake, Pasternak, Lermontov, Mayakovsky, Velimir Khlebnikov, Paul Eluard, Andrey Bely, Alexander Blok, Voznesensky, Asadov, Gutseriev, Anna Akhmatova, Tsvetaeva, and others. Where if the philosopher had not come, the poet would have been there. Poets are like rays of light showing the way to thinkers.

5.782. Syntalism is the philosophy of the 5G generation.

Small thoughts are the philosophical system built in the millimeter wave range. Syntalism is 5G philosophy in the millimeter wave range built according to generative genetic algorithms.

5.767.

In Variothoughts, conceptualization follows the generative genetic algorithm.

5.768.

Variothoughts is the self-teaching guide on generative philosophy.

10.22348.

Syntalism is a philosophy that connects the unconnected with the goal of achieving integrity. Integrity is truth. To know the truth, the mind must cultivate tolerance and humility.

5.783.

Variothoughts is structured as a phased antenna array that ensures a dynamic horizontal and vertical growth of thought according to the generative algorithm and makes it possible to create different-sized logic data arrays. This solution minimizes energy consumed to maintain the integral information field. Variothoughts is a system of small cells in the millimeter wave (super-small thought) range in which the size of cells and their interaction structure are dynamic in nature.

10.3109. Unified system of knowledge.

The philosophy of Syntalism is by far the most perfect and clear philosophy, revealing the nature of being. Syntalism is like an ocean containing all other philosophies and religions. Syntalism understands and explains any point of view, agrees with everyone and loves everyone, considers everyone beautiful. Thousands of points of view, uniting into streams and rivers, turn into an ocean of Synthism.

Variothoughts Collectible Books

4.3423. Sand vs truth?

A book's collectable from the Variothoughts series costs only 1 cubic meter of real estate property. It is a very delicious price for something priceless.

3153.

God loves collectors as they give work to many creators...

6.6033.

The electronic version of Variothoughts is huge but printed versions are more complete and this book's collectables and handmade versions are unique in their completeness. Each of the author's gift manuscripts of Variothoughts is handmade and customized, that's why it includes even the latest texts that exist only in rough copies and have not yet been published anywhere.

10.22513.

Friends, I have not sold any Variothoughts collectibles yet. Pride rules people, that is cowardice and greed. There are very few courageous and intelligent people. He who is brave and buys the first book is very lucky. The first collector's copy of Variothoughts is a great value. Each collection book is registered and numbered. However, there will never be many of them, if I sell such books at least a few pieces a year, it will be good.